CAN'T STOP THINKING

How to Let Go of Anxiety & Free Yourself from Obsessive Rumination

NANCY COLIER

New Harbinger Publications, Inc.

Publisher's Note

NEW HARBINGER PUBLICATIONS is a registered trademark of New Harbinger Publications, Inc.

Distributed in Canada by Raincoast Books

Copyright © 2021 by Nancy Colier
New Harbinger Publications, Inc.
5674 Shattuck Avenue
Oakland, CA 94609
www.newharbinger.com

Cover design by Sara Christian

Acquired by Elizabeth Hollis Hansen

Edited by Gretel Hakanson

Library of Congress Cataloging-in-Publication Data

Names: Colier, Nancy, author.
Title: Can't stop thinking : how to let go of anxiety and free yourself from obsessive rumination / Nancy Colier.
Description: Oakland. CA : New Harbinger Publications, [2021] | Includes bibliographical references.
Identifiers: LCCN 2020047115 (print) | LCCN 2020047116 (ebook) | ISBN 9781684036776 (trade paperback) | ISBN 9781684036783 (pdf) | ISBN 9781684036790 (epub)
Subjects: LCSH: Negativism. | Anxiety. | Criticism, Personal. | Intrusive thoughts. | Self-acceptance. | Mindfulness (Psychology)
Classification: LCC BF698.35.N44 C65 2021 (print) | LCC BF698.35.N44 (ebook) | DDC 158.1--dc23
LC record available at https://lccn.loc.gov/2020047115
LC ebook record available at https://lccn.loc.gov/2020047116

Printed in the United Kingdom

24   23   22

10   9   8   7   6   5   4   3

"In this delightful book, Nancy Colier shows very clearly how addiction to thought is responsible for most human suffering. Clearly our fundamental nature as awareness is intrinsically free of thought. Read this book and experience the freedom to create your reality."

—**Deepak Chopra, MD,** author of *Total Meditation*

"I, too, can't stop thinking, and I'm a meditation teacher who's been meditating daily for over forty-five years! But not to worry. In *Can't Stop Thinking*, Nancy Colier helps us clearly understand how to loosen the tight grip of mental grasping and fixation which brings so much stress. She shares the secret of inner freedom and self-mastery to be able to do what's good for us without self-imposed limitations."

—**Lama Surya Das, the American Lama,** author of *Awakening the Buddha Within*

"One of the most liberating blessings we can receive is the realization that we are not our thoughts! *Can't Stop Thinking* reminds us that, as we learn to meet our mental stories with a patient, forgiving, and wakeful presence, we awaken to the mysterious and loving awareness that is our true home."

—**Tara Brach,** author of *Radical Acceptance* and *Radical Compassion*

"What would life be like if we could recover from our addiction to thinking? We've reached the limit of stress and confusion by believing 'I think, therefore I am.' Nancy Colier helps us take one of the most important steps in life, to realize 'I am not my thoughts.' This is not 'stop thinking,' but ways to break the addictive habit of 'picking up the first think.' What a gift!"

—**Loch Kelly,** author *The Way of Effortless Mindfulness* and *Shift Into Freedom*

"Nancy Colier asks the question, 'What do you miss, and miss out on, because you are consumed by thinking?' With practical exercises and insightful stories, *Can't Stop Thinking* leads us through an exploration of our minds and ultimately to awareness and understanding."

—**Sharon Salzberg,** author of *Lovingkindness* and *Real Change*

"A warm, insightful, and precise guide to making sense of the trickier parts of the human mind."

—**Ethan Nichtern,** author of *The Road Home*

"Rather than fighting with our thoughts, Nancy Colier teaches us to step back from them into a more calm, aware, and nonjudgmental witness space. From this space the thoughts lose some of their hold on us, and we can discover who we really are. Colier's methods are a stand-alone approach to thinking, but also a wonderful complement to other psychological and spiritual practices, including meditation and mindfulness."

—**William L. Mikulas, PhD,** professor emeritus
in psychology at the University of West Florida,
and author of *Taming the Drunken Monkey*

For my girls, Juliet and Gretchen

Contents

Foreword

I can still remember the day I realized that my thinking was driving me crazy. As an aspiring academic in college, I believed in the value of the mind to create realms of complex thought that could solve all humanity's problems. But in my own life I had no control over my own thoughts, and I found myself obsessing about a new relationship to the point that I was so anxious I could barely eat or sleep. Did she, or didn't she? Would she, or wouldn't she? The doubts and negative scenarios my mind churned out had sucked all the joy out of life.

So I finally did what I had contemplated doing for years, since I had begun studying the spiritual traditions of the East as a freshman. I took a subway downtown to a traditional Zen center and embarked on the practice of meditation. Little did I suspect at the time that this was the beginning of a lifelong dedication to the spiritual life and to discovering how we can free ourselves from suffering and live happy, peaceful, awakened lives.

It took me years of following my breath and watching my thoughts as a good Zen student to gradually gain a little distance from the obsessive ruminating that plagued me. In those days there were no shortcuts, no readily available guidebooks on the nature of the mind, no one to say simply, "Look, snap out of it, you're not your thoughts"—in other words, no books like this one. For *Can't Stop Thinking* distills a lifetime of wisdom, gleaned from the author's own meditation experience, her teaching of others, and her decades of counseling clients on working with the mind, into a concise how-to manual for disidentifying from your thoughts and finding peace and contentment in the present moment, without years of meditation.

As Colier suggests, we're addicted to our thinking and believe we can't enjoy life without identifying with the endless stories the mind churns out. Indeed, we take this complex narrative to be who we really are, the truth of our being as a separate self, and we're afraid of what life might be like without it. Sure, we may be suffering mightily, but we firmly believe that the suffering is an inevitable result of what's happening outside of us, what others are doing to us, what life is imposing upon us, rather than seeing it as optional and within our power to regulate. We may even have an allegiance to our suffering because we believe we need to atone for the mistakes we've made, shoulder the legacy of family pain, and learn the lesson it's trying to teach us.

Colier invites us to kick this addiction and forswear this allegiance by taking a single radical step in a new direction. Instead of blaming circumstances out there—over which, after all, we have very little control—we can turn the finger back upon ourselves and realize that the source of our suffering lies within, in the judgments we make, the stories we perpetuate, the interpretations we project. Life is the way it is, not always pleasing or painless, but we can choose how we respond to it. And the most radical, freeing step of all is to recognize that you are not the content of your thoughts; you are the awareness in which these thoughts arise and pass away.

This realization is the first step on the path of awakening from the dream of separation—what the spiritual traditions call enlightenment. For the past forty years, I've been guiding seekers on the journey of awakening, and this first step is always the most powerful and life-transforming. You are not your thoughts—what an extraordinary insight! When you see this once and for all, you've opened a doorway to a whole new way of being—one that offers the promise of a peace, happiness, and fulfillment that can't be shaken by the ups and downs of life. *Can't Stop Thinking* leads you by the hand through this door, and beyond.

> —Stephan Bodian
> *Licensed psychotherapist, spiritual teacher, founder*
> *and director of the School for Awakening, and*
> *author of* Meditation for Dummies, Wake Up Now,
> *and* Beyond Mindfulness

Addicted to Thinking

It was a magnificent spring morning, and I was walking in the park near my home. Well…that's not really true. I was walking, yes, but not exactly *in* the park. I was oblivious to the colorful flowers blooming, the warm sunshine, the smell of cut grass. I was missing all of it, having disappeared inside my own head, into my personal prison—thinking. No matter how delicious that May day may have been, I wasn't experiencing it; I was trapped inside my mind, obsessing about what was not working in my life. Replaying and rethinking the same problems I'd been replaying and rethinking for years; I was down the rabbit hole of thought.

And then something remarkable happened. My inner lens spun on its axis; instead of being inside my thoughts, I was now the one looking *at* and listening *to* my thoughts. I was now the one the thoughts were talking to. I could see, in the brightest Technicolor, what I was choosing to pay attention to. I was suddenly watching my attention attach to this toxic content, watching it latch onto and lather up my discontent. I felt the insidiousness of my thoughts and a kind of bewilderment and horror at my own inclination toward them. I experienced my thinking as something I was actually doing to myself.

In that moment, I could see that I was the one replaying the same stories of discontent, conducting the same resentful conversations in my head—with the same results: suffering, my suffering. At last, I could really hear my thoughts, distinctly—and recognize how bad they made me feel. I observed my negative thoughts for what they were, a kind of self-administered poison. Then the aha moment arrived: It dawned on me that I could do this differently, this whole *life* thing. I could change what I was paying attention to, turn away from the source of my suffering. Not just intellectually, but at a deep bodily level, I knew that I was creating my experience, and therefore, I had the power to change it. If I was willing to transform the way I related to my thoughts, I could create a radically different kind of life for myself.

Simultaneously, it became clear that no amount of thinking and none of my "brilliant" thoughts were actually going to solve the problem I was ruminating on. My thinking mind had met its match. I couldn't solve this particular problem, not with more thought anyway. Whatever I wanted to get, wherever I wanted to get to…if it was going to happen, it was not going to happen through more thinking. I got it: thinking was not going to bring me the happiness or peace I had hoped it would.

That moment arrived after a lifetime of narrating, analyzing, and making sense of my own and everyone else's experience—all to an audience of one: me. Ruminating on what was bothering me, obsessing about how I would fix it, and describing my experience to myself, over and over again. It came after years spent constructing sophisticated mental narratives on why what was happening in my life was happening and what I needed to do to change it. The clarity came after far too much time spent justifying and defending why I was right, and right to have the experience I was having. Defending all this in the court of my mind. The awakening I experienced came after a lifetime of, essentially, fighting with and trying to control reality inside my own head.

On that day in the park, I discovered a new lens through which to see my life and, with it, a new identity. I had not previously known any way to experience life other than through my thoughts, *as* the thinker. There was no witness, no *me* other than the one who was thinking. I was collapsed into the thoughts appearing in my mind.

Like most people too, I had spent my life trusting that I could think my way into a state of happiness and inner peace, that more and better thinking was the solution to all the difficulties life presented. I had believed that if I worked hard enough, muscled my way through enough mental gymnastics, I could figure out whatever was not right with my world. And once I figured it out, I could fix it.

Normal but Not Okay

For more than twenty-five years as a psychotherapist, I've been listening to people talk about their lives. Every kind of problem, situation, history, and personality has walked through my office door. While the contents of our problems and situations may appear in different forms and levels of intensity, there's really one universal problem at the root of all other problems. At the core, our stress, anxiety, and chronic discontent are caused by one thing: the way we relate to our thoughts. It's our relationship with thought that makes us suffer.

Jane is in a bad marriage. She spends her days and nights (and sessions with me) thinking about what's wrong with her husband and why he's so unlikable. Obsessively, she explains the reasons for her anger, the justifications for why she's right to feel how she feels; she explains all this—to herself and anyone who will listen. When she's not ruminating on her resentment, Jane is obsessing on her own faults—blaming herself for staying in a bad marriage, for not being the feminist who would leave. She is trapped inside a repetitive negative thought loop. She goes to work, takes care of her family, and looks healthy on the outside, like someone living a good life. She has moments of joy. On the inside, however, she feels anxious, agitated, and held hostage by her own thoughts.

Alison is a new mother who's just returned to work from maternity leave. Every moment she's away from her son, she thinks about the thousands of terrible things that could happen to her child: terrorist attacks, SIDS, choking on a Cheerio, and on and on. Sometimes she calls me in the middle of the day, when her thoughts turn to panic. When her mind is not generating death scenarios, she shifts to thinking about the devastation she will feel when the terrible thing happens, how she won't be able to survive it. When she manages to pull her attention away from this imagined horror, she thinks about how despicable she is as an absent mom, about how angry she is at her husband for not making enough money to let her stay home with her child, and endless other resentful thoughts. She thinks excessively and obsessively about the very things that torture and terrify her.

Finally let's consider Ken, who believed he was going to become president of the company he worked for. Unexpectedly, he was let go and has been out of work for nearly a year. Since his removal, Ken has been incessantly thinking about what he did wrong that got him fired, replaying the possible missteps he took along the way (down to the photographs he kept on his desk). He asks me every week why I think he got fired. When he's not ruminating on his professional mistakes, he's thinking about his personal failures and specifically, how ridiculous and deluded he was for imagining he could be somebody important. Ken's thoughts, like many people's thoughts, remind him, day after day, of what he isn't.

While these individuals may sound like extreme examples of excessive thinking or what we sometimes call overthinking, they're actually quite typical of the reality many people live on a daily basis. Excessively and relentlessly is just how we think. Most of us are not thinking about unicorns or rainbows either; we're thinking about the things that make us feel the worst. We feel compelled to think about what hurts, and so we suffer. If you can't stop thinking even when you want to, you're not alone.

Like Any Other Addiction

It may sound ridiculous, disrespectful, or absurd to compare the process of thinking, something so utterly natural, productive, and important, to something so dangerous, destructive, and out of control as addiction. A friend, upon hearing the topic of this book, raised her voice to say, "Thinking is not like shooting drugs or drinking. Human beings think. That's what we do!" Thinking is inarguably useful, necessary, creative, and miraculous. It's what distinguishes human beings from other species. The ability to think is a good thing. Thinking is the source of invention, imagination, problem solving, and organization, to say nothing of putting together a grocery shopping list. So, I am not suggesting that we give up thinking; we couldn't even if we wanted to. This is not an anti-thinking book or a how-to on living a lobotomized life. In fact, I am delighted to be thinking right now as I write these words.

Thinking itself, this natural ability of the mind, is not what causes us to suffer. Thoughts themselves are not inherently problematic. What's problematic is our belief that thoughts require being thought about. What causes us to suffer is our identification with thoughts—the belief that we *are* our thoughts. This is the real issue, and precisely what makes it so difficult for us to disentangle from thoughts and find freedom inside our own mind—our own life.

Are You Addicted?

If you ask most people, casually, if they are addicted to thinking, they will say yes. But if you ask people whether thinking is an addiction, the same people will balk and deny it. Our response to the question when we don't think about it too much, when we answer from the gut, is very different than when we pose the question to the mind, whose job, not coincidentally, is to make thoughts!

Do you find it hard to stop thinking about certain things even when you absolutely want to stop thinking about them? Do you feel like your thoughts control your attention and mood? You're probably addicted to thinking, which means you're normal. And yes, you *can* be addicted to something that's natural and good for you, *can* be addicted to an activity that you enjoy and benefit from, *can* be addicted to something you can't live without. While your thinking addiction may not cost you your job or land you in rehab, nonetheless, your behavior is similar, with results that are similarly redundant, destructive, and painful.

To start, let's consider the aspects of addiction discussed in the American Psychiatric Association's most recent *Diagnostic and Statistical Manual of Mental Disorders (DSM-5)*—the bible of sorts for all things psychological—and apply them to thinking as an addiction. Ask yourself:

- Does thinking, sometimes, negatively impact my overall well-being?

- Has thinking created problems in my relationships?

- Have work or home responsibilities been neglected because of thinking?

- When I notice that I haven't been thinking, do I experience fear or anxiety or a sudden excess of thinking?

- Do I find myself thinking more and spending longer stretches of time thinking?

- Have I tried to cut back on my thinking but not been able to make it happen?

- Do I spend a lot of time thinking?

- Has my thinking led to physical or psychological health problems, anxiety, or depression?

- Have I cut down on or stopped doing activities I once enjoyed in order to spend more time thinking?

- Do I ever look forward to or crave thinking?[1]

If you are like most people, you answered yes to six or seven of these questions. Every person I've ever interviewed, without exception, has said that their thinking, in one way or another, creates problems in their life and disrupts their overall well-being. Whether it's from too much thinking or the content of what we're thinking about, excessive thinking causes problems in our relationships, work, health, quality of life, and overall well-being. Thinking is like any other addiction, except for the fact that we don't think it's an addiction. And also, for the fact that we take breaks between our drink, drug, and food binges, but we don't when it comes to our thinking. We devote ourselves to thinking without pause—from the cradle to the grave.

Remarkably, no matter how much we suffer as a result of our thinking, we keep at it with the same resolute faith that thinking will provide the solution to whatever ails us. We continue doing what we've always done despite inarguable proof that much of our thinking is not productive and actually makes us more anxious, stressed, and unhappy. We keep doing the very thing that harms us while hoping for and believing in a different result. We do what we've always done and get what we've always gotten.

Where Oh Where Is the Off Button?

There's no off button is how many people describe their relationship with addictive thinking. Once we start thinking about a problem or situation, we're unable to pull ourselves away from it. We descend into the rabbit hole even though we don't want to go in there, even though we're aware that the thinking itself is what's making us unhappy. As Jane lamented, "There are times I am literally asking myself, *as* I'm thinking, *Why am I still thinking about this? I want to stop. Why can't I stop?* But I just keep at it."

It can be astoundingly difficult to pull our attention away from negative thought loops. We are physically, mentally, and emotionally *hooked*—intensely resistant to the idea of letting go of the thoughts, no matter how much pain they're creating or how much we hate thinking them. We are at war with our thoughts and ourselves at the same time. The obsessive thoughts feel dreadful, but if we dare turn our attention away from them, we experience a fierce backlash that can feel almost worse than the thoughts themselves. While strange, it seems as if we, at some level, actually enjoy, benefit from, or feel empowered by the negative thoughts. For sure, we are attached to them and unwilling to let go.

Usually, we keep thinking until we're forced to turn our attention to something else that can't wait, a crying child or burning pot, or until we go unconscious, either through sleep or self-medication, which, sadly, is the solution many people are choosing these days. In order to stop the cacophonous noise in our head, we have to anesthetize our thoughts and ourselves in the process. We use external substances to relieve our addiction to this overpowering substance called thought.

And yet, it is apparent that the word "addicted" is also misused, misunderstood, and thrown around with far too much levity. Addicted has become a trendy way of describing any behavior we think we overdo or even enjoy. *I'm addicted to gummy bears. I'm addicted to Netflix. I'm addicted to spin class.* There's nothing light or enjoyable about real addiction. I do not use the metaphor of addiction without deep respect for the reality of it. Thinking can indeed lead us down its own path of self-destruction, a destruction we live privately, in the confines of our own mind, and sometimes, without the visible or obvious consequences that often lead us to seek help.

Who's in Charge?

We must remember this: *when* thoughts happen and *what* they're about are not in our control. The mind produces thoughts like the heart pumps blood or the pancreas generates insulin. It's what the mind does—its job. Thoughts form in mysterious ways in the recesses of our consciousness and seem to appear out of the ether. They certainly don't ask our permission to enter into awareness. The reality of constant, random, and unvetted intruders appearing in our consciousness would be challenging enough, but when we compound this truth with the fact that we believe we must also engage with and make sense of each of these unvetted intruders, we end up with a much bigger challenge than just randomly appearing thoughts. We end up powerless over our own attention. As long as our attention is bouncing around at the mercy of thoughts we don't choose, we remain passengers rather than pilots in our own life. As long as our own attention is out of our control, we're trapped on the thinking train, and our life, essentially, is out of our control.

The Fun of It

I recently asked an addict what he feared most about giving up his substance of choice, which in this case was alcohol. Without a moment's hesitation, he said that if he stopped using, he would never have fun again, never have sex again, never go out with friends again, never enjoy life. His life would be utterly mediocre, joyless. Indulging, as he viewed it, was the key to excitement and a *happening* life. The thought of a life with less thinking is similarly perceived as empty or boring. One client described it as a "life without spice, bland, dull…a void." Another asked, "Without thinking, why be alive?" From inside our thinking addiction, we can't imagine what could make life interesting without our stories and drama, all the yummy by-products of our thoughts.

When I told people I was writing a book about our universally shared addiction to thinking, I was frequently met with a sense of outrage: "That's ridiculous…how would we get anything done if we weren't thinking?" "Nothing is possible without thinking!" Or, as one friend retorted, "So then, I should face a blank wall and hum *Om* for the rest of my life? Life is short…I want to be *in* it!" Their reactions imply that, without our perpetual thinking, we will be left in some sort of vegetative state, unable to take action or *do* anything. It is as if the very possibility of life occurring depends upon our thinking.

Exploring this topic has shown me how provocative and unwelcome the idea of doubting the veracity of our thoughts, of disidentifying with them, really is in our society. Contemplating the act of thinking as something we do, not as something we are, appears to be deeply threatening to us. *Not* thinking suggests a kind of death. Given the complexity of what thinking represents, we ferociously protect our relationship with it. To that end, most of us employ a sophisticated array of beliefs about why we should never and will never give up our love affair with thought, even when evidence suggests our thinking is hurting us.

In truth however, we are not to blame for our relationship with thoughts. We relate to thoughts the way we've been taught to relate to thoughts—as profoundly important bits of wisdom that deserve and demand our rapt attention. We kneel at the feet of all our thoughts as if they contain the answers to all our questions.

Recovery

Why are there so many books written on the topic of thinking: negative thinking, overthinking, binge-thinking, and all the other kinds of thinking that create stress and unhappiness, and leave us feeling power-less? Why do the theories and solutions to our thinking addiction keep coming? And furthermore, why is thinking still such an epidemic problem?

Most of us believe that if we could only change our bad thoughts to good ones, write enough gratitude lists, repeat enough affirmations, then we would be happy. Most of us think it's our fault that our mind over-whelms us so much. We must not be doing the right work or enough of it. But the truth is, it's not our fault. We don't recover from our addiction to thinking through the strategies most self-help literature advises. We don't have to like our thoughts to be free. Self-help is solving the wrong problem.

Recovery from excessive thinking is *not* about stopping thoughts or achieving a thought-free existence. At the same time, it's not about changing what our thoughts are *about*, skewing our thoughts from nega-tive to positive. Although this can be helpful, it's not the solution. Recovery happens when we change the way we interact with thoughts, the value we assign them, the belief we invest in them, and the attach-ment we have to them—no matter what contents or messages they contain. We recover when our allegiance shifts from being aligned with the thoughts and their content to being aligned with the one who the thoughts are talking to (or at), which is what you'll be learning more about in the pages to come.

This book is here to help you build a safe shore, a refuge inside your-self, from which to see and interact with the thoughts appearing in your consciousness. My hope is that with this new awareness, you will be able to cultivate a more conscious and intentional relationship with thoughts. All this, so that you can be content regardless of what the out-of-order computer in your head is spitting out at any given moment. This book is designed to show you how to break free from the compulsion to turn every thought into an occasion for thinking, to stop worshipping at the altar of your mind. My goal is not to help you find freedom *from* thought but rather to find freedom *with* thought. Thoughts are not going away; they're not going to go away. (We wouldn't want them to anyway.) My purpose here is to illustrate a way to be free and autonomous...*while* your thoughts are firing. And most of all, to shepherd you into the well-being and peace that is inside you, and always there—below the thoughts and thinking.

Breaking your addiction to thinking requires falling out of love with the endless material your mind generates without your consent. This process involves a willingness to recognize what your excessive thinking is actually doing to you, the suffering you are creating for yourself. And, how your thinking choices (or lack thereof) are impacting the quality of your life. The good news is that your thoughts don't need to change one iota for you to be released from them, or rather, to release yourself from them.

A Good Life

While we have a sophisticated educational system, oddly, we don't learn the most important skill we need to maintain a basic state of well-being. In order to create and sustain a good life, we must cultivate a conscious and constructive relationship with our own thoughts, a relationship that allows us to use thinking for the delicious benefits it offers—but that doesn't permit thinking to take over our life or wreak havoc on our experience. We have infinitely more choice than we know when it comes to our own attention and what we do with it. We are not powerless when it comes to which thoughts we take a ride on. We don't have to live at the mercy of the thoughts our mind throws at us, which is positively not what our mind wants us to think.

A glass of wine can be used as a lovely treat at the end of a long day, but that same substance can be used as a means to flee from our life, avoid the present moment, inflict self-harm, fulfill an obsession, or any number of destructive ends. This is true of our thinking as well. When we think without awareness, discernment, and discipline, we give up control of our life. We give away our own attention, and with it, the authority to decide our state of mind and being.

Throughout this book, I will lay out the subtle and not-so-subtle consequences of excessive thinking, which, if you are old enough to be reading this book, you have probably experienced firsthand. I'll explore the infinitely complicated conundrum that the activity of thinking presents—what it does to us when we let it control us and what we can do about it. But most importantly, I'll provide the tools to build a new and empowered relationship with thoughts, one in which you are in charge—not your thoughts. In so doing, I hope to offer liberation from your universally sanctioned addiction—lasting relief from the real source of your chronic discontent. In the pages that follow, I wish to invite you into a life in which thoughts do not control the most precious asset you possess—your own attention. And furthermore, a life in which your thoughts are not the truth and, most definitely, not who you are.

A New Way of Living

We live in a society that demands and expects immediate answers: strategies to implement for life's challenges. We want relief from our suffering—understandably. And indeed, this book includes exercises to help you break free from the unending thinking that causes you to suffer. But unfortunately, you can't just think your way out of excessive thinking or you would have been free of this addiction years ago, and your life would be radically different. Trying to think your way out of excessive thinking is a recipe for even more thinking.

The best way to change your life is to change the you who's living it. When the eyes you're looking through change, what you see changes. The observed is changed by the observer. When who you are in relationship with your thoughts shifts, so too will your life experience.

I encourage you to let the words on these pages soak in, to let the meaning be absorbed by your body and heart, not just your mind. It's strange what I'm asking you to do—to think about thinking and at the same time to experience these words through a different portal than just your thinking mind.

I invite you to suspend judgment and resist the urge to think too much about how to *not* think or to think more about thinking less. Try experiencing the journey of this book in a new way, not knowing what it means immediately and just letting it wash over you. As odd as this all may sound, try not to get it all figured out too soon. Your own path to freedom from excessive thinking will emerge. For now, trust that the way you see your thoughts *can* shift, that *you* can shift in relationship with your thoughts, that your thoughts may indeed become *thoughts without a thinker.*[2]

My hope is that this book will be helpful for you no matter where you are in your life—whether you've never meditated or have been practicing awareness for decades. Know that this book will be more helpful if you have the courage to listen to your own experience as you read it. And… *most* helpful if you're willing to refrain from thinking it out of its helpfulness.

If you picked up this title, chances are some part of you wants to ruminate less, stop catastrophizing, turn off your thoughts when you want to turn them off, have more choice in what you think about, hear less noise in your head, feel less anxious, experience more peace, or maybe all of the above. Perhaps you already know that the way you think is making you unhappy and that changing your life will mean changing your thinking. The good news is that you're right. The even better news is that it's possible. I'll make one promise to you in this book: if you change your relationship with thinking, you will change your life.

CHAPTER 1

Awareness: Changing Our Relationship with Thought

Tara came to see me when she was in her midthirties. By her own account, she had devoted the last ten years of her life to conquering and eliminating her obsessive and, as she called it, unstoppable thinking. She had been devoted to self-help for a decade and tried anything and everything to convince her mind to "stop talking" and, specifically, to stop telling her she was worthless. Mostly she had used positive thinking methods, which included affirmations and gratitude practices. She had worked hard to change the thoughts she heard in her head. She was a self-help pickle by now—no longer a cucumber and no going back. But, here she was in my office, still struggling and stymied by her unceasing inner chatter, feeling hopeless and beaten, powerless over her thoughts and powerless over what they were doing to her.

I've met hundreds of Taras—people who have been disappointed by self-help and psychological fix-it strategies. My practice is filled with folks who were unable to find lasting relief from their excessive thinking through the self-help techniques that forever beckon and promise us a new life. If you also have tried everything on the shelf, don't despair. It's not your fault that you haven't found what you need. Controlling the content of our thoughts is a temporary fix, a shiny hat over dirty hair. It works, to some degree, when things are running smoothly and we like what's happening in our life. But when the going gets tough and life rolls out the hard stuff, which it always does at some point, the positive thoughts don't stick. The fix-it strategies fail, and we revert back to our old belief systems and historical thinking patterns. Positive thinking can be helpful, and it feels good, but it doesn't get at the real problem; it's not strong enough to create real change in the beliefs that underlie our negative thoughts. Ultimately, it's just a Band-Aid on a far deeper and more powerful condition.

What makes positive thinking an inadequate solution is not just its unreliability. The real reason it falls short is that it's addressing the wrong problem. When the strategy is to replace negative or unwanted thoughts with positive ones, we are relying on misguided beliefs, assuming the following: we can and should be able to control our thoughts, what our thoughts are saying is important, our thoughts have the power to control us, and finally, we have to get our thoughts under control before we can be okay. All of which are false. Positive thinking maintains (incorrectly) that our well-being depends upon what our thoughts are saying at any moment, and thus our successful management and control of the thoughts are the keys to our happiness. In this system, we are still at the mercy of the contents of our thoughts, still dependent on what is not ours to control. Positive thinking claims to empower us but, at the root, it disempowers us.

Self-help sells a kind of cognitive ammunition, an arsenal for winning the war against our unwanted thoughts. But, if what you want is to not feel controlled by your thoughts, then the answer is to stop trying to control your thoughts—stop trying to defeat them. What frees us from negative thinking is not winning the war against our thoughts (over and over again, minute by minute, day by day, for years on end), but rather, removing ourselves from the war altogether.

Stepping Out for Peace of Mind

So then, how do we step out of the battle? What is the strategy for surrendering the fight? The process I'm suggesting begins with a radical shift in perspective. The positive thinking system says that in order for us to be okay, our thoughts have to be okay—to our liking. This suggests that we are reliant upon our thoughts. Essentially, it says we *are* our thoughts. But what if this is not true? Stepping out of the battle with your thinking starts by considering that your well-being does not depend on correcting thoughts at all, and furthermore, does not depend on your liking or even agreeing with your thoughts.

Have you ever noticed, when thoughts are not here, even if it's just for a moment, that you are still here, still awake, still conscious? We remain, with or without thought, which strongly suggests that we are not made of our thoughts. How can we still be here if what we are is not here? As you'll experience repeatedly through the exercises in this book, sometimes we can see our thoughts happening, see them actually arising and even passing. The fact that we can see our thoughts, and hear what they're saying, also tells us that we cannot *be* our thoughts. We can't be what we can see happening in front of us. It turns out that well-being depends upon our realizing that we are *not* our thoughts and our thoughts are not *us*.

Ask Yourself: *What if I am not my thoughts? What if I am what hears and sees the thoughts, the awareness within which thoughts are appearing?*

Let this possibility germinate in you; walk with it, sit with it, shower with it, eat with it…notice what happens.

Thoughts appear and disappear within our field of awareness, that much is true. We, however, are not responsible for their content. Thoughts can say what they want and will, and we can still be okay. Our thoughts stop controlling us when we cultivate a separate place inside ourselves from which to observe thoughts and when we stop seeing it as our job to correct and conquer them. Freedom dawns through awareness, specifically, the awareness to see what's happening inside your own mind, as an observer. And it begins by surrendering the responsibility for controlling what you see.

Awareness Is Observing

I discuss awareness a lot in this book. And indeed, awareness is the key to breaking free from addictive thinking. But "awareness" is a word we throw around to mean many things. It's also something we don't think of as a skill, but instead as something we just possess and are born with. To some degree that's true, but in the context of this conversation awareness is something very specific and a skill we must develop and cultivate.

Awareness, as I refer to it, is the practice of creating an inner witness who can see thoughts without being identified, merged, or collapsed into them. Before you can make any choices about how you want to relate and respond to thoughts, you must develop an "I" or a witness who's separate from thought. You need to step back, as we can't change our relationship with something until we can see it as "a something" we're in relationship with. As Eckhart Tolle explains, once we can see our thoughts, we're no longer addicted.[3]

Seeing Thoughts Like Birds in the Sky

When we're born, we experience life through our senses. There is seeing, hearing, tasting, smelling, and feeling, but not yet a *me* who is doing all that. Sensing is just happening; our self, our experience, and our environment are all one thing. But as we grow and start to see and experience ourselves as a separate entity, a *me* with a name who shows up in the mirror, and then the proverbial *my* tummy, *my* candy, *my* wheelbarrow, *my* mommy, ad infinitum, we start to experience ourselves as separate from our environment. That separate *me* then, over time, is conditioned to focus on the objects appearing in his or her awareness: toys, things, people, food, and so forth. *Oh look at that, touch this, taste that.* Our attention is consumed by the thing we're pointing at. But in the process, we've lost sight of the seeing or sensing itself: *the awareness that makes relationship with the object possible.* We've lost contact, simultaneously, with the space within which the object appears.

If you point at the sky and ask, *What's that?* most people will tell you a bird, an airplane, a cloud, or some other object they see at that moment within the sky. But what goes unseen and unexperienced is the sky itself. We are so trained to focus on the thing appearing that we miss the infinite space, the sky within which the birds, planes, clouds, and all the rest come and go. Such is the case with our mind. We perceive only the thoughts, but not the awareness out of which they arise and into which they disappear. We hear only the words, but know nothing of the one who hears the words. To change your thinking, however, you must become aware of the awareness that surrounds thoughts like the sky hosting the birds.

EXERCISE: THE BASICS OF AWARENESS PRACTICE

Awareness, for our purposes, is simply noticing what's happening—and that's it. Being able to do this is a skill that you can cultivate by practicing paying attention to this present moment, on purpose, and without judgment. That is, you can become more aware of what's happening in your mind, body, environment, and everything else the present moment contains. You can notice what's here now without deciding why it's here, whether you like it, or what you need to do about it. You basically observe without getting involved in the contents or story lines being offered. When you practice awareness, you adopt an attitude of curiosity and friendliness; your goal is to simply look without looking for anything in particular.

1. Imagine that you are pointing a camera at your mind right now. What do you hear and see?

2. Observe what's happening in there—inside your head. Are there lots of thoughts or just a few here and there? Are the thoughts distinct so you can make out the particular words or images they carry, or are the thoughts appearing more like a background of static and noise?

3. What's the mood of the thoughts? How do the thoughts feel (without going into the content)?

The purpose here, oddly, is not to answer these questions. These questions are just pointers, or guides, to help you witness your own thoughts without doing anything to change them. These inquiries are about one thing: learning to stay still and watch the movie of your own mind.

When we practice awareness, sometimes referred to as "mindfulness," we turn our attention inside ourselves and observe. We don't make a story about what we see, don't try to figure it out or fix it, and don't try to attain anything through it. We just look, without changing, improving, managing, or controlling what we're seeing. While it sounds quite simple, ridiculously simple even, and maybe even pointless, it is anything but easy.

The most effective awareness practice, ironically, is the simplest, almost too simple for the mind to be able to understand, or bear. It's a practice that purposefully starves the mind of its usual diet of strategies and improvement plans, homework assignments, lists, and things to do—things the mind can busy itself with. Awareness practice is absent the strategizing our mind relishes and without the mental gymnastics to which we are accustomed. The mind gets squirrely with so little instruction, so little to do; it wants to get busy judging, story-making, and planning to change what it sees. But we do our best to stay still and just look.

This practice is one of observation as its own destination, to take the seat of the witness in and to your own mind. It's as if you set up a camera and point it at your mind, but then walk away from the camera as it films the field in front of it. The filming is happening, but you are not there to judge, interpret, or edit it. It's like the French style of "truthful cinema," or *cinéma vérité*, with the subject being our own consciousness.

What I have described is awareness practice in its purest form: just looking at your thoughts and being curious and friendly. If you are new to awareness practice, however, it may feel impossible to just look at what's happening inside your mind without any agenda or strategy and without any plan for what your mind should do with it. That's okay. If you try it, but still feel it's impossible to be without an intention other than to observe, you can give your mind something to pay attention to—a way to busy itself while you practice *not* being your thoughts.

EXERCISE: RESTING ATTENTION ON AN OBJECT

In awareness practice, the breath can be used as an object of attention, an activity of sorts for your mind (a bit like throwing a puppy a sock to chew so she stops crawling all over you). The breath works so well, not because it holds any important or mystical qualities, but simply because it's always here and always available as a doorway into now.

The practice is this:

- Focus your attention on the sensation of the breath, whether at the nostril, chest, or belly, wherever it is most distinct. (Where you notice the breath is not important.)

- Notice and feel the inhalation and exhalation, and the subtle pauses between them.

- Do this even as your thoughts are coming and going, and beckoning (like mad) for your attention.

As you sit and pay attention to your breath, and simultaneously resist the urge to get involved with the content of your thoughts, to go on the rides they offer, you are cultivating a *you* that is not made of thought, a *you* that can decide whether or not you want to engage with thought.

1. Close your eyes and take a deep breath.

2. Place your hand on your abdomen and take another breath, paying attention to the sensation of your abdomen rising and falling.

3. Bring your attention inside your body and notice any sensations present.

4. Now let your attention rest on your breath. Feel the sensation of the breath, wherever it's most distinct.

5. There's nothing to do, nothing to control or change in any way. You're simply noticing and feeling the sensation of the body

breathing itself. Keep your attention on the individual breaths, one at a time.

6. When sensations arise, notice the sensations, but keep your attention resting on the breath. When thoughts arise, notice the thoughts without getting involved in them and without judging yourself or the thoughts. Keep your attention on the breath.

7. If you notice you've trailed off into thought, notice that you've been absent and, once again, return your attention to the breath. Don't judge yourself for thinking; just come back to the next breath.

8. Continue this practice for ten minutes if you can. You may have to return your attention to the breath a hundred times in these ten minutes, and that's normal. Every time you realize that you've been lost in thought, not present, celebrate the fact that you woke up and became aware of your own absence.

As you stay with the breath and notice the thoughts arising without getting involved with them, you are building the muscle of awareness, disentangling yourself from thoughts—de-identifying from the contents of your mind. And, with time and practice, you start to experience *yourself as the awareness* to and within which the thoughts are occurring, rather than as the thoughts themselves.

When you sit down to practice mindfulness, what's important is not what you find in your mind when you observe it, no matter how interesting or revolutionary it may be, to you. An astrophysicist once shared that a scientific breakthrough had appeared to him in a meditation session; he experienced an epiphany that would change our understanding of the universe. But the mindfulness teacher responded with a wave of his hand, utterly disinterested in these findings. He reminded the scientist not to attach to or celebrate what was appearing in his consciousness, the contents of mind, but rather to just look and notice what was doing the looking—the awareness.

This is an act of curiosity about your own consciousness—not about the material that you discover there. You stay anchored to the breath as you notice the movements of mind. The idea behind this kind of practice is to observe your mind from a place that is not thought. Rather than seeing *from* your thoughts, you are looking *at* your thoughts, *from* the awareness that notices them, but is not *of* them.

Establishing a Regular Practice

The most important thing about awareness practice is that you do it and do it consistently. If you really want to break free from being controlled by your thoughts, I suggest a regular—daily, if possible—practice. Remember, as many years as you've been alive is how many years you've been feeding your addiction to thought, taking every thought to heart, and believing that you are your thoughts. It takes time and practice to peel yourself and your identity away from thoughts, to have the awareness muscle it takes to really look at them and yet not be seduced by them. Thoughts are seductive; that's just true. Consistency and commitment in our practice are therefore necessary in order to build the strength and presence it takes to resist their seduction.

If you can, spend a minimum of ten minutes each day practicing this kind of mindfulness, just paying attention to what's arising in your field of awareness—thoughts and sensations. If you can do twenty or thirty minutes, even better. If you can only eke out five minutes on a day, practice for five minutes. This is not a competition, not an all-or-nothing thing; whatever time you can devote to awareness is beneficial and time well spent.

You can do it on a chair, meditation cushion, yoga mat, or sofa. Sitting up straight, in a good posture, can help formalize and deepen your practice, but it's not what's important. What's important is that you practice, period. So too, you can practice awareness anywhere: on the subway, at your desk, in a restaurant...your location is irrelevant. And in fact, the minutes you practice don't even have to happen all in a row. If you just can't get ten minutes in sequence (which is its own problem you might want to address), then take a couple minutes here and there to stop what you're doing and turn the lens of awareness around so it's pointing at your own mind. It's helpful, as well, to practice awareness in a more general style. Without any formality, you can just keep an eye out for what your thoughts are up to and how they're affecting you.

Nonjudgmental Seeing

Awareness can also be developed through the practice of nonjudgmental seeing. Our thoughts are made up of opinions, likes and dislikes, interpretations, analyses, and judgments. The practice of nonjudgmental seeing, on the other hand, is the exercise of experiencing life, even if it's just for a moment here or there, *without* adding our opinions and judgments onto what we're experiencing. If it sounds radical, it's because it is; it's the complete opposite of the way most of us normally live. In nonjudgmental seeing, we practice being in the present moment without supplementing it with our thoughts about what's happening. Our experience simply happens, and we refrain from formulating a set of ideas *about* it, what it means, and all the rest. We live it without the whole commentary that usually accompanies it.

EXERCISE: NONJUDGMENTAL SEEING

While it may sound inconceivable to live without constant opinions, the practice of nonjudgment is actually not that hard to get the hang of. However, it can feel very strange when we first start, given the fact that we've spent our entire lives formulating thoughts and opinions about...well... everything.

1. Close your eyes and take a deep breath through your nose: bring the air all the way down into your belly. Hold the inhalation, and then breathe out a long, slow exhalation through your mouth. Hold the exhalation. Do this a few times (or more if you'd like).

2. Scan through your body and notice whether there are any places of constriction or tension. Offer these places an invitation to relax and release what they're holding. Take your time.

3. Now open your eyes and look around the room. See what you're seeing, but refrain from internally commenting on it. Don't name what you're seeing, decide whether you like it, decide what needs to be done about it, or do anything else for that matter. Just look... take in what's in the space without language and without knowing anything about it.

4. Notice what this experiment evokes in you.

Without our opinions added on, life feels different. Still rich, but just different. Through this practice of nonjudgmental seeing, we start to taste a way of experiencing life that's not defined by judgment and commentary, you might say, not lived through our thoughts. When we give ourselves permission to live without having to come up with a narrative or an opinion on what we're living, our addiction to thinking naturally eases. As a result, we end up feeling profound freedom and the deepest relief.

No matter what's happening in your day, you can always stop for a moment and observe the kinds of thoughts passing through awareness. You can maintain a certain level of attention, all the time, to how your thoughts are impacting you. Awareness practice is more than just something you do; it's a way of being with yourself and indeed a way of living. This shift in attention, lived and practiced regularly, will deliver profound results and, ultimately, free you from chronic discontent.

As you move through this book, you will find a host of awareness practices, as well as deepening tools for common thinking patterns and conundrums. Beneath all awareness practice is the intention to break free from our attachment to thought and to know ourselves as more than just thought. Awareness is the simplest practice we will ever do and also the most powerful. Why not start today?

PART I

Styles of Suffering

CHAPTER 2

"I Obsess About What Hurts the Most"
Thought Loops and Rumination

Have you ever noticed how much time you spend thinking about what went wrong, is wrong, and will go wrong? If the answer is a lot, you're normal, even if it doesn't feel normal or good. According to a study by the National Science Foundation, humans experience as many as sixty thousand thoughts per day.[4] Deepak Chopra, MD, sets the number even higher—between sixty and eighty thousand thoughts per day.[5] Furthermore, according to current research, 80 percent of those thoughts are negative, and 90 percent are redundant; that is, they tell us the same things over and over again.[6] Oddly, the more negative a thought, the more we're inclined to engage with it and return to it. If you do the math, that's a lot of negative and repetitive thoughts.

When a thought appears, we instantly are off on the ride it offers (or threatens). We view its invitation as a mandate and jump on board without consideration—no matter where it's headed. Indeed, thinking can take us on some dangerous rides and into some dark and dreadful neighborhoods inside our own mind.

Pamela wakes up every morning inside what she calls "a hornet's nest." Before her head is off the pillow, she's deluged with swirling thoughts like "venomous wasps," an unending stream of problems to solve, things that might go wrong, and tasks to be completed. She starts her day flooded with anxiety, dread, and a sense of overwhelm—before her feet even hit the floor. "It's like being engulfed in a swarm of bees, thoughts buzzing all around and inside me." It's as if our mind wakes up with all the stored-up energy it didn't get to release for eight hours. It returns to consciousness by aggressively producing thoughts and reestablishing its place as commander in chief.

The Evolutionary Function of Negative Thoughts

At an evolutionary level, we focus on the negative as a survival instinct. As psychologist Dr. Rick Hanson explains, we have a negativity bias when it comes to our attention. Negative information creates more activity in the brain, more firings than positive information of equal intensity. Our brains are also better at noticing the negative than they are at noticing the positive. In an effort to protect us, our brains exaggerate threats, undervalue our abilities and strengths, and obscure our capacity to deal with difficulty. "We're Velcro for negative experiences and Teflon for good experiences," says Hanson, which means we think about, remember, and deem important whatever goes wrong or is bad in our life. And, at the same time, we tend to forget, discount, or minimize what's good.[7] What's certain is that we have a harder time unsticking from negative thoughts once they've got their glue on us. Bad glue is stickier than good glue.

Compounding the problem is the fact that negative experiences take up more space in our brains than positive experiences. Dr. John Gottman, a relationship researcher, discovered that for each negative interaction that takes place between a couple, it takes five positive interactions to bring that couple back to a state of contentment. In terms of importance, it's a five-to-one ratio, positive to negative—an uneven fight indeed.[8]

For millions of years, living creatures have had to decide whether to focus on either getting the things they want or avoiding the things that could hurt them, what Hanson calls "chasing carrots or ducking sticks."[9] When it comes to avoiding extinction, ducking the stick may be a better strategy. After all, if we miss the carrot today, we can probably find one tomorrow, but if we fail to duck the stick today, there won't be a tomorrow. Evolutionarily, it's wiser then to keep our attention vigilantly attuned and scanning for those elements that could potentially wipe us out of existence.

Modern Dangers Are Different

Our understanding of what constitutes danger, "the stick," has changed since the time of jellyfish. In modern times, the threat of dying in the forest at the stroke of a stick has been (for the most part) eliminated. With 412 varieties of cereal to choose from at our local grocery store, the drive to survive biologically has been replaced by a drive to survive psychologically. It's the psychological death from which we seek to protect ourselves now. Our minds are working around the clock to keep our self-worth, our ego, from being injured or annihilated. With the real-life carrots and sticks gone, the potential threat shifts to our identity—the story we tell ourselves about who we are. We're always scanning and strategizing to ensure that no situation damages our value or self-esteem. While I'm sure there were many sticks to avoid when we survived in the forest, in modern times, the potential threats to our ego are infinite. As a result, hypervigilance seems to be mandatory when it comes to keeping ourselves psychologically and emotionally intact.

At the most basic level, we return to our negative thoughts because we're trying to turn a negative experience into something more positive, essentially, to make it come out a different way. Our mental replays are attempts to rescript an experience we *don't* want into something we want, to reestablish our self-worth and emotional balance. If we could just understand our negative situation better, know our problem more clearly, spend more time with it, eventually, we'd be able to make it disappear, or at least feel better. We hold tight to our pain so we can figure out how to make it go away. We believe an answer exists inside every negative situation, and if we could unearth it—through thinking—it would free us from pain.

A Painful Paradox to Self-Care

Clinging to suffering, paradoxically, is a way of trying to take care of ourselves. We're convinced that the kernel of resolution will appear from somewhere inside the rubble of the problem. But usually the only thing that appears is more suffering…we're left stuck in the rubble, scavenging for that unfindable gem of relief.

So too, continually thinking about what hurts makes us feel that our pain matters, that it didn't happen for no reason, and that it won't be forgotten. We refuse to steer our attention away from what hurts because doing so feels like abandoning our pain, and thus abandoning ourselves. We stay with our suffering to keep our suffering company. As a client, Morgan, expressed: "It's so painful to turn away from what hurts, even more painful than it is to think about or feel it." When we think about leaving our pain behind, a great sadness can arise, as if we're making the choice to ignore our wounds, to turn a deaf ear to their truth, our truth. To stop engaging with thoughts seems to say that our pain doesn't matter or, maybe worse, is not real.

Our ruminations provide our suffering with empathy, which so often it doesn't receive from those we most want it from, those we think have created our pain or should care. To stop revisiting our hurt can feel like we're moving on before the hurt has been properly heard, validated, or soothed. In this way, our attention (in the form of thinking) can feel like a salve to our wounds.

I had known Sharon for many years before she lost her child in a car accident. For the decade that followed, she talked about her child every time we met and about how she couldn't live without her daughter here on the planet. Her pain had been excruciating since the accident. Understandably. At one point I asked her, with the deepest compassion, who she would be if this were not at the center of every moment of her life. She told me that she didn't want to be anyone else. She didn't want to move on. If she didn't think about her daughter, her daughter wouldn't exist, and she couldn't allow that, would never survive that. She told me, without question, she would rather suffer every moment for the rest of her life as opposed to move on from this. For Sharon, it couldn't be over. She wouldn't let it be over, ever.

You might hold onto your suffering because you're not ready for the past to be past. You may not feel ready to let go of what the pain contains and also not ready to let go of the hope that your past could become a better past. We return to our painful thoughts and memories as a way of coming home to ourselves, returning to a core self-experience. Pain can feel deeply familiar. It may be how we felt in our families growing up. Pain, in its own way, can be comforting—it's what we know, a state of being that feels like home. As a felt experience, pain has a weight and depth that is grounding, calming even—as opposed to happiness, which can feel light, ephemeral, and untethered—without roots. For many people, pain can actually feel safer than happiness.

While we can acknowledge that focusing on our pain may have a self-caring intention, nonetheless, we must also acknowledge that, in practice, it does not take care of us. You need to give proper attention to your wounds—no one can skip this step—but you also must recognize when you've acknowledged and felt your hurt *enough*, spent enough time honoring it. You don't have to live *in* or *from* your pain in order to know it or take care of it. Pain will present itself when it needs to. It will arise organically when you're in it, but you're not obligated to bring pain into this now when it's not naturally here. You don't *need* to wallpaper the present moment with suffering in order to prove that it matters.

EXERCISE: IS THINKING HELPING OR HURTING?

This practice can help you discern when your devotion to your pain, when keeping company with your suffering, is no longer helpful or self-loving and when you compulsively and habitually scratch at your wounds. All of us have to decide when enough is *enough*.

1. The next time you're caught in a painful memory or thought loop, stop for a moment and place one hand on your heart. Feel the kindness in this simple gesture, of inviting your own heart into the space. Take a deep breath.

2. Ask yourself—with curiosity not judgment—*Have I sufficiently acknowledged the suffering that this particular situation has caused me?* If not, take a few moments and offer yourself that acknowledgment, that compassion. Remind yourself that this matters. Say it out loud.

3. Then ask yourself whether going over this situation again—retelling this story, revisiting what hurts, rehearsing the case against whomever harmed you—is actually easing your suffering. Is it coming up with a solution? Is it changing what happened? Is it making you feel better? If it is, then by all means continue, but if it isn't, then give yourself permission to stop.

While turning away from your painful thoughts can feel counterintuitive, unloving, and even retraumatizing, in fact, more often than not, it's the very thing you need to do to feel better. So take genuine care of yourself and do this practice; take this moment and give yourself a chance at contentment.

At first, it can feel like you have to gather up all your strength, brace yourself, and rip your attention away from painful thoughts, like a bandage off a deep cut. But, every time you shift your attention in this conscious way, every time you decline pain's invitation and refuse to engage with painful thoughts, you're doing three important things:

- Loosening your attachment to negativity and suffering

- Building the muscle that you use to direct your own attention

- Cultivating a sense of self that's separate from your thoughts, a place from which you can be *with* your thoughts, in a relationship with thoughts, but without being identified or merged with them

It is the idea of what it means to leave your pain behind that hurts— your thoughts about leaving your thoughts, *not* the actual leaving, and certainly not what's left when they're gone. Despite the rumors our mind may proliferate, when we peel our attention away from what hurts, we don't feel abandoned, uncared for, or invalidated—all the things we feared would happen. Our negative thoughts are not missed. As it turns out, if we don't hold onto our pain, our pain doesn't hold onto us.

Suffering is left behind, but not in the way we imagine, not like an abandoned dog on the side of the road. To dismiss thoughts of pain is not to dismiss pain. Whatever you've lived, every experience and emotion, has become a part of you, integrated into the fabric of who you are now. The *you* who turns away from the painful thoughts and turns back to the present moment already contains the experiences you're trying so hard to hold onto. You don't need to constantly remind yourself of the pain to keep it. The pain won't suffer when you stop rigorously attending to it. It isn't waiting on the side of the road for you to come back and get it.

When we're not engaging with our painful thoughts, life can positively surprise us. We're more present and open to new experiences. The relief we've been longing for is right here under our nose. As one friend described, "Who knew I could choose to say no to the pain and yes to the present moment…that something so direct and simple would be the solution." We tend to spend our whole lives looking for a way to fix the past so we can have permission to enter the present, only to find out that we didn't need permission at all. The whole paradoxical catastrophe is tragically ridiculous.

Wounds Can Become Who We Think We Are

No discussion of our attachment to pain would be complete without a mention of pain as a part of our identity. Pain is profoundly intertwined with our sense of who we are. What we've endured, overcome, and survived: our struggles, challenges, sorrows, and losses—our scars—make us *us*. Our difficulties do become a part of us. They change us. Our suffering is integrated into our nervous systems, hearts, and brains. And yet, negative experiences take up a disproportionate amount of space in our sense of who we are. We're deeply attached to our stories of suffering—we *love* our pain and take pride, strength, and solace in what we've suffered. Our pain defines us; it's the meat of our self. We habitually think about our pain as a way of experiencing ourselves. Ending your love affair with your pain, therefore, can feel like you're giving up who you fundamentally are.

Ask Yourself: *What am I afraid of…if I stopped reminding myself of my pain, of what I've survived? Who would I be without my suffering?*

If it feels right, you might also want to journal (preferably with pen and paper—not on a screen) with this exercise.

Jim's mother was, in his words, "critical and unsupportive, totally unable to celebrate me or my talents." As Jim experienced it, she was never proud of him and never enjoyed anything about him. As an adult, he frequently thought and talked about the absence of a proud mother in his life.

Over time, Jim had built a strong narrative of himself, one that he spent much time ruminating over and used to explain whatever wasn't working in his life. He thought of himself and related to others as the guy who'd been unsupported and uncelebrated, who could have been so much more, who could have realized his great potential—had he been encouraged. Jim had locked himself into the role of someone who didn't get what he needed and deserved.

Noticing how much time Jim spent thinking about his mother and what he had lost out on, I asked him, "What would you have to give up if you released that whole story, resigned from your role of *that* guy—if you stopped thinking that past experience with your mother back into the present moment?" His answer, after a moment of reflection, was insightful and pointed, "Who would I *be* if I weren't the guy who wasn't enjoyed by his own mother? And maybe worse, what would I have to do if *I was responsible* for fulfilling my own potential?" While he said this with a smile, we both understood the dire truth in his hypothetical questions.

EXERCISE: WHO AM I NOW?

For a single conversation or even a whole day, try showing up for life as someone with no history, no narrative. Notice what it's like to live without a story, without a preconceived idea of who you are and what's happened to you. Drop "before now" and let there be only "now." Notice who you are (or become) in the absence of a self-story. Notice how it feels to be free of your story on you.

It turns out, when we stop continuously reminding ourselves of who and how we are, often, we are surprised by what we discover. Who we are turns out to be *not* who we think we are and who we keep telling ourselves we are. Without the heavy coat of a predetermined self, the present moment appears light, naked, alive, and ripe with potential. At last, we can meet what's here without our story of self in the way.

Keeping Busy by Chewing on Mental Junk Food

Perhaps most importantly, we feel drawn to difficulty because it gives our mind something to do. A problem is an activity, a task, a free pass to kick up as many thoughts as possible, all in a valiant effort to help us find a solution. Giving the mind a problem is like giving a dog a bone. The mind gets to analyze it, contemplate it, play with it, make pro and con lists about it, talk about it, and for as long as we'll let it (which is usually pretty long), chew on it. As far as the mind is concerned, there's nothing's as fun and empowering as a big, juicy problem. If the mind celebrated Christmas, it would ask Santa to bring it a sleigh full of problems! Every day!

When things are going well in our life, however, there's not much for the mind to do or solve. We can think about what's going well and maybe even think about how grateful we are for it, but there's not much else for the mind to do with happiness or contentment. Confronted with a state of well-being, the mind gets antsy and nervous, and quickly comes up with a plan. Soon enough, we find ourselves with a new bone in our teeth, busy thinking about how we can protect what's going well from going bad or going away. We're thinking about what it'll be like when what's good is gone. How dreadfully bad that will be. From there, we can get thinking about all the things we need to do to keep this good thing going. It's a path without end, a bone that can splinter into an infinite number of baby bones. Great news for the mind, as it gets to stay fully engaged and employed.

As we become more familiar with our thoughts, however, it's important that we do not demonize their presence. Thoughts are simply a part of the human experience. They cannot *not* exist. It's not their fault or our fault they're here. Even our negative thoughts, in their own misguided way, are an attempt to protect, defend, and guide us. While they may fail dreadfully at fulfilling this intention, and, in fact, end up working against us, we can still recognize that much of our thinking is motivated by a desire to make us feel better and keep us safe. Changing our relationship with thought, paradoxically, includes offering compassion to the very thing from which we must also separate and disengage.

CHAPTER 3

"What's Wrong with Me?"
Self-Criticism and Negativity

When it comes to negative thinking, we humans have an endless array of thinking styles to choose from, a plethora of stress-inducing thinking loops into which we can pour our attention. Amidst the abundance of negative thought options, however, we tend to skew toward certain favorite flavors.

Our number one favorite thinking loop is the one that specializes in *what's wrong with me*. This kind of thinking is so popular it has its own famous author: *the inner critic*. With this voice narrating in our heads, we spend vast amounts of time, more than the ten thousand hours supposedly required to master a sport or craft, thinking about our faults. We're experts at identifying and formulating the myriad ways we're broken, lacking, unlovable, guilty, to blame, and just plain not good enough. It's odd that we willingly spend so much time and energy thinking about what's wrong with ourselves, rehashing our failures, stoking our shame, and reliving the most awful moments of our life. How can this be our favorite choice for thinking? And yet, we do, and it is.

Peter, an intelligent, attractive young man with a great sense of humor, is forgiving and nonjudgmental—with other people. He saves up his anger and disapproval for himself. Highly self-critical, Peter relentlessly reminds himself (and me, his therapist) of his mistakes, of his inadequacies, and how he's not what everyone else thinks he is—unless they think he's bad, in which case he is what they think he is.

In our society, self-criticism is the form of negative thinking that we suffer from the most. It is downright normal to beat ourselves up with our thoughts. If we don't do it, we're strange. Whole sections of bookstores are devoted to solving this kind of thinking, but the troves of advice don't seem to be solving the problem.

The Misguided Protector

Odd though it may sound, at the inception of nearly every self-critical thought lies some form of positive intention, no matter how twisted, faulty, or outdated. Rarely have I found an exception to this rule. In Peter's case, when I asked him what he would risk were he to stop reminding himself of his failures, he said that his criticisms made him get things done, and without them, he'd get lazy. He was sure that if he stopped building a case for his flaws, he would forget them, get cocky, and start blindly acting them out. The positive intention within his negative thoughts was born out of this belief that his thoughts made him better and protected him from his inherent inadequacy. From this perspective, thoughts were there to help him.

Identifying the beliefs behind your self-critical thoughts can be revolutionary. Once you can see the beliefs, you can unravel them, unearth their faulty nature, and thus strip them of their power. I asked Peter if he would test out his theory, namely, that attacking himself motivated him to accomplish more. When he returned a couple weeks later, he was smiling and told me that he had discovered something mind-boggling. He noticed that when he stopped reminding himself of everything he'd ever done wrong, he felt freer, lighter, and happier. Consequently, he was able to get more things done and be more productive. He said it felt like he had taken off a ten-thousand-pound coat. Rather than having to approach every new experience as a test to prove his self-critic wrong, a chance to *not* fail *again*, he had permission to do what he needed to do—to attend to the tasks in front of him, and no more.

Peter's self-critical thoughts had convinced him that they were there to whip him into shape—that he needed whipping in order to function well. But what he discovered was that without them, he was filled with energy and good ideas, quite the opposite of what he had feared. When he stopped believing his negative thoughts, Peter's life became possible: He was free to function well in the present moment. He didn't need whipping after all. Have you ever given yourself a chance to find out whether your story is really true? Are you willing to give yourself that chance?

Identify a specific criticism or judgment you hold against yourself.

Ask Yourself: *What is the belief (about me) behind this self-critical thought? If I were to let go of this judgment, what do I fear would happen? Who or what am I afraid I would become without this thought? What story about myself is this thought supporting? From whom did I learn this story about me?*

Once you've unpacked the self-judgment, where you learned it, and what its purpose might have been, you can consider leaving that suitcase on the side of the road or maybe handing it back to the person who packed it for you. Notice who you are without it. Right now is the time to forgive yourself for whatever crimes and mistakes you think that negative version of yourself committed. This is the moment to break the cycle, release what you were taught to believe about you, what you thought kept you safe. Who do you want to be? Be that person—starting now.

Disappointed So We Don't Get Disappointed

Self-critical thoughts, in their own illogical way, are also an attempt to protect ourselves from negative feelings. We tell ourselves we won't get what we want, can't expect to get what we want, and shouldn't even bother trying, all in an effort to protect ourselves from feeling disappointed, ashamed, and inadequate if things don't go our way. We set ourselves up for defeat so we're ready for defeat (should it come). Essentially, we force ourselves to pre-experience disappointment and self-loathing to protect ourselves from disappointment and self-loathing. But telling ourselves we won't get what we want usually ends up preventing us from getting what we want. We've already taken ourselves out of the running, or if not entirely out of it, we're carrying a heavy backpack of negative thoughts that weighs us down and makes it less likely we'll achieve our goal. The more we try to protect ourselves from feelings of failure, the more we ensure that we'll fail.

By inserting our assumptions of disappointment and failure before reality has been written, we're conducting a mandatory dress rehearsal, compelling ourselves to preemptively run through the negative feelings. If it turns out that indeed we don't get what we want when the time comes, we'll then have to live the feelings a second time—for the real show. Will the real feelings sting any less because we got to feel and rehearse them ahead of time? No, they will not. By setting ourselves up for disaster, in advance, all we end up accomplishing is an extra experience of suffering.

Why make ourselves experience these negative feelings twice rather than once, or maybe even not at all? Why not wait and see whether we need to experience disappointment or shame even once? And if we do need to, why not live them when they're actually called for? Why not save the experience, whatever it may be, for when the feelings are real and not imagined?

When we tell ourselves we're going to fail, what we're really doing is trying to control the anxiety of not knowing what will happen. Once we decide we're not going to succeed, we've solved the problem of the unknown. We've inserted a negative conclusion and no longer have to live in what's unknowable, and as yet unwritten. We're not going to get what we want, case closed, anxiety (and uncertainty) successfully avoided. We can thus understand the self-critic for what it's really up to, namely, trying to help us escape our desperate discomfort with uncertainty.

The antidote to this self-destructive and self-discouraging thinking is to remind ourselves of the truth: we don't know what the future holds. We don't know whether we will or won't get what we want.

Ask Yourself: *Do I want or need more practice experiencing disappointment or shame? Am I willing to stay open to the uncertainty and* *acknowledge that I don't know what will happen—that uncertainty is the only real truth? Am I willing to accept that the story hasn't been written yet?*

Remember, you're writing the story of your life right now. As you think it, so you create it. Rather than generating a fictional failure, we must remind ourselves that we don't know, and indeed, no one knows what will happen in the future. What is helpful in the face of the unknown, in the unwritten story, is to show up with grace, try our very best, be the person we want to be, and have the courage to live directly in the discomfort. We can live in the not-knowing without imaginary answers.

Maintaining a Status Quo

In other instances, our self-critical thoughts are sneakily designed to protect and maintain a certain status quo. When I met Melanie, she was an actress with a powerful but slippery inner critic who was forever telling her that she was just a mediocre performer. When she had a chance to land big roles, this critic would open fire with a deluge of thoughts reminding her that she was *not* one of the special people, not someone who was ever going to be a star. This voice whispered that she was the dependably average one, a hard worker, but not a real "player." Always there in the shadows, the thoughts were poised to pounce on any opportunity that could lead to a change in who she thought she was. It was clear, however, that her inner critic's story simply didn't match her personality, her talent, or the response she was receiving from the rest of the world.

Cleverly, Melanie's thoughts didn't accuse her of being untalented. Their story on her was more nuanced and to some degree, more insidious—not the kind of inner critic you immediately recognize as damaging. As I got to know Melanie, I simultaneously (through her accounts) got to know her mother, also a performer, who demanded a lot of attention and "was always the brightest light in the room."

I asked Melanie what a relationship with her mother might be like if she, Mel, became a *special* person, famous or successful. She shook her head, let out a big "ha," and said, "Not sure she'd be up for that challenge…supporting actress…to her daughter, no less." After a bit, she got more serious and sad, adding that she just couldn't imagine that happening. There was no room for another star in the family. Melanie's thoughts had found a way to protect her from having to live that unimaginable scenario. As devoted as her mother, on the surface, was to supporting her daughter's career, it was evident that Melanie's success would have gravely threatened her mother's role, which, consequently, would have threatened her mother's ability to be supportive and loving. Mel knew that either she got to have a mother or she got to have a career, but not both. Her thoughts supported her choice for a mother and ensured that Melanie would get what she needed most.

Our negative thoughts, as hurtful and destructive as they can be, may also contain profound intelligence. It's usually an intelligence born out of a younger and less psychologically well-developed incarnation of ourselves, a coping mechanism that was necessary at a time when we had less awareness, insight, and resources.

Ask Yourself: *What early experiences or family dynamics inform my self-thoughts? Are they helping me maintain the status quo, maintain the same me? Do I still need these thoughts working behind the scenes on my behalf? Do I still want this reality?*

What matters is that we become aware of the deeper beliefs our thoughts are operating from and consider whether such thoughts are still acting in our best interest. Once the roots of our thoughts are unearthed, our choices and actions become clearer and easier.

The Negative Caretaker Inside

Sometimes our self-attacking thoughts are simply a matter of repeating to ourselves what we heard from our caretakers growing up. Having internalized our caretakers' negative versions of us, we continue to talk to and think about ourselves in the ways we learned were appropriate and deserved. If, from an early age, we were taught to believe that we deserve blame and criticism and aren't worthy of kindness, then that's what we tell ourselves and how we treat ourselves.

By internalizing our negative caretakers, repeating their words and sentiments, we keep an active relationship at play with those caretakers. We are saved from having to examine the choices and behaviors of those people who taught us to believe such negative thoughts about ourselves. In so doing, we can keep our caretakers *good* and us *to blame* because the idea of our caretakers, the people who are supposed to love us, being wrong or profoundly flawed is too painful and discordant to accept. We adopt their version of who we are so we don't ever have to recognize that their words and actions may have been unwarranted, unkind, unsupportive, untrue, or not what we needed to thrive—even if they were doing the best they could. We are saved from having to confront the possibility that those who we needed to love us were not always loving. Taking on the negative voices of our early influencers, we ensure that we'll never have to experience the unfairness—the tragedy—at the very root of our own negative thoughts.

EXERCISE: A COMPASSIONATE TONE

No matter what you think is true about yourself, no matter what you've been taught to believe, take a moment to feel what it's like to go through life with this story about you.

1. Place a hand on your heart and imagine yourself at the age when you started believing these negative thoughts about yourself.

2. The practice is not to consider whether you deserve the criticism, to validate or invalidate it, but to simply feel what it's been like to continue this kind of relationship with yourself. What has it been like?

3. Imagine that you're speaking to that child—you—what would you want to say? What would that child have wanted to hear? What words or actions would have really helped at that point in time?

4. What words or actions will help you now?

The goal here is to cultivate kindness for yourself, for the self that was and is being judged and criticized, the self who, even worse, was taught that it deserves it—that *you* deserve it.

Even if you still think you deserve the negative thoughts, if you can feel a hint of kindness for yourself, simply for having to live with the belief that you're bad, not enough, or broken, then you're steadfastly on your way to a new relationship with your self-critical thoughts. When such thoughts arise, rather than identifying with the attacker and jumping on board, you can shift your identification—from the one who's doing the attacking to the one who's taking the beating. From this new perspective, it is obvious that self-attacking thoughts are no longer welcome and can no longer be tolerated.

Is It True?

When you listen closely to your self-critical thoughts and tune in to what they're actually saying to you, you'll likely notice that a lot of it is simply false. It doesn't match up with what you say and do, how you behave, and ultimately, who you are, even by your own estimation. Most of us would disagree with some of what we habitually tell ourselves about ourselves.

If you think that everything your critical and judging inner voice says is absolutely true and irrefutable, then inquire as to whether anything else is *also* true. If negative thoughts are telling you that you're selfish and self-centered, ask whether you are also, some of the time, generous and giving. Perhaps you can remember a time when you were not selfish or self-centered.

When we're caught in a thought loop, we're operating in a good-or-bad system. But the truth is, we're all good and bad, lovely and not—contradictions at play. In a word, human. So expand your vision to include more of yourself, a more realistic and (dare I say) forgiving view—the whole picture, not just one tiny piece or moment of it. You can, essentially, pull the lens out and away from where you're fixated.

As a human being, you're inherently and inescapably imperfect. When identified with self-critical thoughts, you've revoked your right to be who you fundamentally are, have condemned your basic nature, and are sparring with an unconquerable and disinterested opponent called "reality." Whether you're willing to admit it or not, you are a work in progress, doing the best you can, even when it might not be your best on another day or the best you can imagine in your head. Whatever you do *is* your best at that moment because it is what you did or said or were, despite everything else you knew and *could* have done. Even if you were aware of another choice, a better choice, or if deep down you knew it was a bad choice, you chose what you chose. This confirms, without exception, that you were not ready or able to make that other, wiser-known choice. You didn't have it in your wheelhouse just yet.

Our best is not what we think or know is best, but what we have the ability and power to carry out. Our best in any moment is determined by what we actually do—not what we know or think. As flawed creatures, we sometimes act in ways that don't represent who we want to be and can be. When we make a mistake, miss the mark in some way, what matters is that we identify and unpack the mistake itself: We investigate what led to it, what thoughts and beliefs created it, and most importantly, what is to be learned from it. We acknowledge the mistake, take responsibility for our part, make amends if necessary, and drop it.

Let me repeat that. We acknowledge the mistake, own it, make amends if necessary, and drop it. We let the mistake be what it was, and no more. Don't add a story line to it or expand it to become a testimony of your self-worth, proof of why you're bad. Mistakes need not be character assassins. Mistakes can simply be opportunities for you to become more self-aware, to keep progressing as the work in progress that you are. They can simply be mistakes and, ultimately, teachers.

The fact that you fall short doesn't mean you're bad; it just confirms that you're imperfect, which hopefully you already know. Even though there's no other way we can be, we still refuse to forgive ourselves for our basic nature. To recover from self-critical thinking, hammer home to yourself, regularly, that your goal in life is progress, not perfection. The important thing is not that you've missed the mark—that's merely a blip on the screen, your starting place—but rather what you do with that truth, how you change and evolve, how courageous you are in your forward movement. It comes down to being more mindful and self-aware, which we'll cultivate throughout this book. Every moment we spend lamenting our missteps is another moment of life we've effectively thrown away, another opportunity we've squandered, when we could have been behaving in a different way, being and becoming the self we want to be.

What Would They Say?

When we're inside the hornet's nest, getting stung by self-critical thoughts, we can invite a friend into the nest with us; that is, we can imagine what someone who loves us, a friend or trusted teacher, might tell us in that moment. Sometimes, the kindness or fairness that it requires to break out of a self-critical loop can only come through inviting in another person's experience of us, seeing ourselves through another set of eyes.

EXERCISE: INVITE A KIND VOICE

At the moment you're hooked, you may not have access to a loving or realistic view of yourself. So, imagine what a respected other would say to or about you and—no matter how ridiculous or seemingly untrue—force yourself to hear it. The act of unhooking from your own thoughts and inviting in this more balanced and compassionate version of yourself can change the internal weather and reroute your self-critical loop.

1. Place a hand on your heart. Take a deep breath. Tune in to your own felt experience.

2. Now call to mind someone who loves you, from any period in your life, alive or dead. Someone who makes you feel cared about, whom you trust wants the best for you, wants you to be happy. Invite the kindness and love they feel for you into your own heart. Imagine soaking your inner critic's words in this kindness.

3. Say to yourself inside, "May I experience kindness. May I feel loved. May I be happy."

Repeat these words out loud if you can. Write them down. Put a list of them in your pocket and carry them with you. This way, you can learn a new way of relating with yourself.

We don't come into this life with self-hating thoughts. We learn them. We're taught them. When you catch yourself joining forces with the self-critic, you can stop and acknowledge that *you* are now the one doing to yourself what was done to you, *you* are now the one making the choice to perpetuate this self-inflicted unkindness. You can also remember that this self-attack is positively not organic or natural. You don't have to do it. There is no reason to do it.

Awakening to the tragedy of this learned, self-critical relationship with ourselves is the real path to releasing the self-critic. Once we actually care about ourselves and our heart breaks for our own suffering, we can't beat ourselves up in the same way. It's just not possible. Compassion for our own experience is the true antidote to self-harming thoughts.

CHAPTER 4

"What's Wrong with Everyone Else?"
Grievance, Resentment, and Blame

If we took a random snapshot of our attention at any given moment on any given day, there's a strong chance we'd find it comfortably entrenched in thoughts of how to control and change the people, places, and things in our personal world. We love to ruminate on the people, places, and things responsible for our life not being the way we want it to be, the way it *should* be. We delight in rehashing all that's to blame for our discontent. It's a negative thinking loop that rages against grievance and assigns blame—in a word, it is our complaints.

This particular flavor of negative thinking was my personal favorite. When I relapse, it's still my flavor of choice. I spent more time than I'd like to acknowledge rehashing the situations and people I was most bothered by: how certain people were blocking me from being happy and what I needed to do about it—how I was going to fix it. I argued many cases in the courtroom of my own mind—proving why my frustration, anger, and discontent were justified—why it all made sense.

I missed a lot of present moments, lost in this tsunami of what I didn't like and what I was going to do to change it while life was passing me by.

Railing at Others Harms Us Most

Each time a situation arises that we don't like or agree with, we are convinced that this is *the situation*. This issue is at the core of our suffering. If we could solve and control *this one*, get the other person to understand—and change—what they were doing wrong in *this situation*, then we would be happy and free, then we would be done with having to control and fix our situation, then we would be okay. Unfortunately, every grievance is *the* one, and we wouldn't dare let go of any of them. We never get to the bottom of the pile. The time never actually comes when we can stop trying to control and fix our situation.

When we're trapped inside a blaming loop, we're shoring up our convictions about what's causing our suffering—solidifying our rightness and the other's wrongness. Essentially, creating our own hell. With all our righteous rightness, we succeed only at building ourselves a cage of anger, dissatisfaction, and victimhood in which we then have to live. We've proven our airtight case against the other but at the expense of our own well-being. The other person, situation, or institution may be wrong as we see it, but we're the ones suffering—no matter who's to blame. We keep lighting ourselves on fire, hoping the other will die of smoke inhalation.

An Endless Search for Pain Relief

So, what are we trying to accomplish with all this self-inflicted suffering? Is there a positive intention anywhere in this painful process? Yes. Obsessively rehashing our grievances is a primitive and flawed attempt to make ourselves feel better. In relentlessly thinking and talking about who and what that we didn't like, we're trying to understand what happened and get it into a narrative that feels manageable. Through our replays, we're trying to transform a negative situation into something acceptable, trying to get okay with what doesn't feel okay.

Our complaining thoughts are simultaneously an attempt to empower ourselves. We feel aggrieved, mistreated, or bad, and so we puff up our chest with our righteous indignation and chime on about how wrongly we're being treated. It's a way of proving to ourselves and whoever will listen that we're deserving of better treatment. We matter and should not be treated this way. We keep thinking about it until we prove it to ourselves, which sometimes never happens. When we're feeling small and life feels unfair, we focus on who's to blame—how we're right and they're wrong—all in an attempt to feel less victimized, bigger, and better.

Ruminating on what's causing our unhappiness is an attempt to contain and compartmentalize what hurts. If we can get the right conceptual packaging around our hurt and anger, we'll be able to get it into a tidy box, put it on the shelf—and keep it there. If we can understand and explain what's making us feel bad and why, the hope is it might not feel so bad.

When we're busy griping to ourselves, we believe that somewhere in this rabbit hole of complaints, maybe way down at the bottom of it, we'll find the relief we desperately crave. But, the more we scratch, the itchier (and bloodier) it gets. The deeper down the rabbit hole we plunge, searching for relief, the farther away we get from it.

In some elementary way, we're wired to obsess over what's bothering us because, as the spiritual teacher Eckhart Tolle suggests, we associate complaining with getting what we want. As children, if we throw a temper tantrum, it will often lead to a change in the situation we're railing against. If we complain loud or long enough, we can usually wear our parents down so we get what we want. As adults, we operate within this same framework. If we whine enough about our situation, eventually, the situation will change. Someone somewhere, maybe the universe or God, or the other person involved will do something to make it better for us, as it happened in the past. But because it's no longer our parents we're fighting with (who presumably care about our unhappiness, or at least, don't want to have to listen to it), because it's now reality we're pleading with, a reality that isn't interested in our complaints and can't be worn down, we're fresh out of luck. Our endless complaints remain within us, against us, and against reality—useless when it comes to improving our situation.[10]

Rehashing our grievances is an attempt to get our suffering heard and understood. By obsessively revisiting what feels unfair, we're providing ourselves with an undivided and unconditional audience for our complaints, something we don't often receive from those we believe should care. In serving as an ear for our own suffering, we're offering ourselves validation, concern, affirmation, and, ultimately, love. Our grievances are grieved within the presence we desperately crave, one that never grows tired of our upset.

Yet, despite the positive intentions behind our incessant self-complaining, we benefit more when we take a good look at whether it is accomplishing our goals.

Ask Yourself: *Is it true that I feel more validated as a result of thinking about what hurts? Is it true that I feel more empowered from thinking about what's unfair? Does thinking about my discontent free me from my discontent? Do my angry thoughts transform my anger into something more peaceful?*

If you're like most people, the answer is a clear no—all around.

Fighting Reality Internally Doesn't Change It

Like the Greek God Sisyphus, who was condemned for eternity to roll a giant rock up a steep hill only to have it roll back down each time he neared the top, we mortals chase after a life in which everything is exactly the way we want it to be. But like Sisyphus, we never actually get to the top of that mountain or create that life in which we agree with, or are pleased with, everything and everyone. As soon as we are pleased with one thing, another thing falls apart, and so life goes. The bad news is that life will always continue being life, with its joys and sorrows, irritations and satisfactions. The good news is that when we change our mind, change our relationship with our thoughts, how we experience life's *lifeness* also changes.

Furthermore, when our attention is focused outward at what we think is making us miserable, we're perpetuating an unhealthy dependence on external circumstances. The belief that our well-being is at the mercy of our situation leaves us powerless and frustrated, in a constant state of fragility because we can never control our external reality. Convincing ourselves that the rest of the world is forever the cause of our internal agitation leaves us desperately trying to control everyone and everything, to orchestrate a life that always goes our way—in other words, a life that doesn't exist. As long as we're focusing on what's wrong with our external world, we're perpetuating our own misery.

There's only one thing I know that's true 100 percent of the time. When we fight with reality, reality wins. We use our grievances as weapons to fight with reality. True to form, reality wins, always, which means we lose.

Freedom from your grievance-focused thinking becomes possible when you discover that your internal fight with reality has not and is not going to change it. When you stop living in a state of aggression with the way things are—bracing against what is—you discover acceptance and a different level of peace. It doesn't mean that you should stop trying to change life when it's not to your liking, but it does mean that you choose to stop fighting against the fact that life *is* the way it is right now—this *is* reality, like it or not.

Whatever is bothering you on the outside (no matter how juicy a problem) is really a doorway into something threatening you on the inside. We change our relationship with our thoughts when we turn our attention away from what our thoughts are talking about—who and what we resent—and turn toward ourselves and our experience. The idea here is not to shift from blaming someone or something else to blaming yourself, but rather to use your aggrieved thoughts as opportunities to get in touch with your own feelings and fears, and deepen your understanding of the real problem.

Once you accept that your suffering is not actually caused by the newest object of your discontent, you're less likely to feel victimized by life situations and less inclined to suffer. When you stop believing the thoughts that are telling you the *other* is the problem, the *other* is what's making you miserable, the *other* needs to change for you to be okay, then the *other* becomes less problematic.

When a complaint or resentment next appears, turn your attention away from the object of your disapproval, from what you think is causing your unhappiness. Look within.

Ask Yourself: *What feelings, hurts, or fears is this situation or person triggering in me? Does this situation put me in touch with humiliation, inadequacy, loss...does it make me feel unloved, unseen, unimportant, or how? What does this feeling remind me of?*

We don't experience suffering; rather, we suffer our experience.[11] Our situation is *not* what causes us to suffer. What I'm suggesting here is not meant to minimize the brutality of what we sometimes have to live through. Our situations can be monstrously challenging; I've walked through situations that were so painful I wasn't sure I could get through them, and likewise, I've accompanied others through such circumstances. More than anything else, what determines whether or not we consistently suffer—whether or not we're okay—is the *way* we interact with our life situations, which ultimately reflects the relationship we create with our own experience.

Your grievances are your teachers—here to show you what your real suffering is about and where your real freedom can be found. Contentment becomes possible when you give yourself permission to stop focusing and fixating on who and what stands in the way of it and get on with the business of creating contentment no matter what anyone or anything else is up to.

By paying attention to your own side of the street as opposed to cleaning up all the other streets in the neighborhood, you will discover that you can be content in a life that includes things you don't like and wish were different. Stop thinking so much about the "problem," taking everyone else's inventory—diagnosing and repairing the *cause* of your discontent. And instead, turn your focus to your own responses and attitude; attend to who you want to *be* in a world that will always be *not* entirely to your liking. Then you can create a good life without changing anyone or anything.

Challenges then become opportunities—to do something different, be somebody different, within it, and stretch beyond your habitual patterns. You can even learn to look forward to problematic situations and people as opportunities to practice being who you want to be—your best self. When you turn the lens back on yourself, you reclaim your power; you regain the right and dignity to choose what your participation in life will be.

Failing Our Way to Freedom

What starts us on the path to freedom is failure. Very little of the obsessive thinking, rehashing, ruminating, rehearsing, proving, scripting, controlling, and mock-dialoguing that goes on inside our echo chambers actually makes much of anything better in the relationships or situations we're obsessing about. Almost none of it creates real change. In fact, our ruminating makes relationships worse, as we are more entrenched in what we perceive is wrong and thus less present and available to what is actually happening. What do we accomplish through all the hours and days spent thinking about what bothers us? Making ourselves even more bothered. We fail ourselves first.

Despite believing at some level that you are helping yourself by searching for solutions to your problems, nonetheless, you're likely also exhausted, bored with your own thoughts, and sick and tired of feeling the way you feel. It's only when you can't stand to keep doing what you are doing, can't take listening to the same story lines, that you'll make a commitment to yourself. As soon as you notice an old (or new) grievance arising, promise yourself you'll deliberately do something different.

EXERCISE: MOMENTS OF CHOICE

The next time you're about to dive into the mud with your thoughts, pause for a moment and make a different choice. Follow these steps.

1. Acknowledge the muddy thoughts themselves. Do not get involved in their content, but consciously note that the complaints are here.

2. Remind yourself that if you follow these thoughts, go for the ride they're offering, you will suffer—this is certain.

3. No matter how compelling and believable the negative thoughts may feel, choose to say no—to refuse their invitation. Say the words out loud: "I will not do this—will not feed this story with my attention."

4. Take a deep breath. Check in with your senses. Corral your attention into the place where your feet are planted.

5. Do this over and over and over again.

It's crucial to initiate this practice as soon as you first detect the rumblings of negativity, to catch the thoughts at the gate, before they gather strength. The longer your thoughts rumble and make their case, the more likely they will hook you in, and then once again you will need to claw yourself out of the rabbit hole. So, start this process early, be consistent, and be fierce.

Through this simple but radical practice, we discover something deliciously surprising. That is, when we consistently turn away from the negative thoughts and stories in our head, we actually feel freer and happier. So too, we feel guided by a greater source of wisdom, and even love. Just the act of making this simple choice for ourselves, for our own well-being, feels like a moment of grace. In the process, we stumble into the realization that we can change our life by choosing how we relate to our thoughts. We, all of us, can create the kind of inner environment in which we *want* to live.

You have the capacity to take this step and make this profound choice. It may not be your first or most intuitive choice to turn away from the negative thoughts that feel so enticing and seductive, as if they'll fix the problem. To stop feeding your unhappiness takes awareness, conviction, and a desire to stop making yourself suffer. Let me repeat that: To stop making yourself suffer. It takes courage to step into the unknown, try something you don't yet know will work, and reject what your mind is saying you *should* think about. The process of turning away and turning toward something different is about your willingness to change—if for no other reason than you're not willing to stay the same.

Wake Up to Your Freedom

This is a process of waking up and seeing, clearly, that you are the one making yourself unhappy. The toxins you are ingesting are your own thoughts. The present moment is usually okay, but you are actively injecting it with discontent. Understanding this truth, fully and irreconcilably, gives you no choice but to stop doing what you have been doing *to* your now and *to* yourself. Waking up to the failure of obsessive thinking as a path to happiness sets us free.

Somewhere deep inside, barely in the realm of the conscious, we believe that letting go of our grievances is tantamount to abandoning our suffering. We believe that we need to directly attend to the contents of our unhappiness, get into the particulars, and solve them. We think that thinking is the only way to find a solution and thereby relieve our suffering. We are wrong. Realizing that more thinking would not and will not solve our problems, we let go and offer ourselves a different experience of life. Ultimately, we stop trying to control and change what isn't ours to control or change. Turning away from suffering, in reality, is an act of profound kindness for ourselves. What we think of as emotional self-neglect, the deprivation of our own empathy, turns out to be just the opposite: an expression of self-love.

Hiding in the most unlikely, counterintuitive place lies the solution to our self-inflicted suffering. Not a solution to the particular problem at hand, the situation we think needs fixing, but a solution for a new way of experiencing life. All this time, what we needed to change our reality was to come back to the reality that was already here. The present moment has been waiting for us all this time, but we have to fail long and hard enough to be able to see it.

EXERCISE: TAKING A BREAK

Choose a problem that you're currently wrestling with...not a traumatic problem, but something that's bothering you.

1. For the purposes of this exercise, give yourself permission to *stop trying* to figure it out. Tell yourself, "Just for now, I don't have to solve this, don't have to devise a next right step." In this moment, give yourself a break from all fixing.

2. Allow yourself to rest in this parenthesis of relief.

3. Notice what it feels like to be off duty from solving the problem.

4. Notice too, that this problem-free space was created entirely by you, and not by any change in the problem itself.

As a practice, refusing the invitation to descend into the rabbit hole of negativity can feel ridiculously simple and easy, too simple and easy to be an answer. The mind prefers and trusts complexity. (The mind and complexity are natural bedfellows.) But the experience and wisdom, born of suffering, that it takes to be able to implement this practice is anything but simple or easy. After the countless hours I spent thinking about how to fix and solve my grievances, here's what I figured out, and I hope this exercise helps you reach the same conclusion: I can't, we can't, feel good with more control or more thinking.

I give you permission (and the strong suggestion) to turn away from the contents of your discontent and rejoin your life, to be where your feet are right now. You're not copping out, bypassing your problems, living in denial, taking the easy path, or abandoning or neglecting yourself. You're actually choosing the path of wisdom and self-compassion when you stop perpetuating a self-generated hell on earth, the one inside your own mind, and choose to be free.

When We Stop

A miraculous thing happens too when we stop obsessively trying to think our way out of problems: our problems tend to become less problematic. And even more amazingly, solutions that we could never have thought up start to appear. When we're deep down the rabbit hole, we can't believe that something other than our own minds can get us out. We trust only our thinking, as we've been taught. But, when we really get it—get that thinking won't take us to freedom, when we finally surrender and accept that we can't mentally muscle our way out of suffering—something else shows up and shows us another way, a way we never could have thought up.

But here's the thing. You can't *do* it. You can only stop trying to figure it out, turn it over, and get out of the way.

EXERCISE: RECALL YOUR MOTIVATION

Offer yourself a simple mantra, which is a saying that is helpful and beneficial to repeat often. You can say it to yourself inside or out loud...once a day or five hundred times a day. It goes like this:

I don't want to suffer. I want to be happy. I want to know peace. I want to be free.

You can change the words around to make it fit just right, shorten it, or lengthen it. But no matter the words, say it and do it. This is a wish for your own well-being, for the end of your suffering. It's a gift that changes your relationship with yourself and thus your relationship with everything—including your thoughts.

Remember, you're doing something radical and new. You are literally resetting your mind's wiring—building new mental habits and pathways in your brain. It takes effort and conviction to rewire the mind; it will not feel natural at first. Your mind will want to pull you back and will come up with all sorts of enticing reasons why you must continue ruminating on your problems. Negative thinking is what the mind has always done. But persevere, hang on tightly to your *no*—remind yourself of where you end up, every time, when you follow your negative thoughts. Imagine your grievances as Post-it Notes, prompting you to come home to your senses, to drop your awareness out of your head and into your body. Remember that you don't want to suffer. Remember, you want to be happy.

CHAPTER 5

"What If Things Go Wrong?"
Fear, Worry, and Catastrophizing

While self-criticism, grievance, and resentment are focused mostly on the past, fear, worry, and catastrophizing are negative thinking projected into the future—ways of paying our negativity forward. Catastrophizing, as the name implies, is creating catastrophes in our mind that don't actually exist in reality—inventing, imagining, obsessing, and suffering over what could go wrong. And, of course, supplementing and accessorizing those imagined catastrophes with what we must do to fend off or recover from them.

As a likely catastrophizer himself, author Mark Twain captured it well when he reportedly said, "I am an old man and have known a great many troubles, but most of them never happened." We experience so many awful and terrifying situations, spend years actively living through one disaster after another, and yet, much of the horror we experience hasn't happened and won't happen in real life. It doesn't exist anywhere but inside our own mind.

Ramona is a fourth-year medical student and a classic catastrophizer. Since she entered med school, she's been worrying about and planning for what will happen when she fails her medical boards. She thinks about what restaurant she'll wait tables at and whether she'll end up homeless as a result of her student debt, with no way to pay it back. Ramona lives out these imaginary scenarios as if they were really happening.

Back in reality, Ramona is in the top 5 percent of her medical school graduating class. The probability of Ramona failing her boards is close to zero. And yet, when in the grips of catastrophic thinking, reality is not a factor in determining what the future holds or what's true. The mind is insistent on preparing for the worst and scariest possible outcome, which no matter how unlikely, is still considered certain.

So many of us self-inject fear into our nervous system. We force ourselves to live the worst when it may not happen and definitely has not happened. Why, when given a blank slate and unknown future, do we choose to write a story of catastrophe and terror?

Facing the Unknown

As is the case with self-critical thoughts, which convince us of the certainty of our failure, catastrophic thoughts convince us of the certainty of a disastrous future. Once again, the thoughts stem from feeling out of control and anxious in the face of uncertainty, the uncertainty of what the future will actually hold. Faced with the predicament of an unknown future and nothing to do about it, we inject the situation with something we're more comfortable with, something we know—the certainty of doom. Once we know it's all going to go badly, we've solved the real problem. And, as an added bonus, our mind can now get busy with its favorite activity: worrying about and planning for the disasters headed our way. The anxiety of the unknown has been successfully replaced with the far more understandable anxiety of what we have to do about the impending catastrophe.

Some people, when faced with the discomfort of the unknown, choose to fill in the unknown with a gloriously positive story. It's going to be a huge success; we are going to get everything we want and more. And yes, if we're going to think up a story about the future, why not invent a fabulous one rather than a horrific one? But, if we genuinely want to be free from excessive thinking, we need to accept that neither story line, not the positive or the negative one, is actually true; the future is unscripted. Both story lines are efforts to create a sense of control. Our *what if* when it comes to the future is really just a replacement for the *what*? *What* will it be? We don't know. There's nothing for us to do with a reality that's not yet a reality. We can't micromanage what doesn't exist. We just have to wait in the not knowing.

The more lost you are in what-if thinking, the more you need to pull yourself out of the future and ground yourself in this moment, now—in the choices you're making today. This begins with being able to accept feeling uncertain.

There is an urgency to practicing "I don't know" because when we've convinced ourselves the future is a disaster, we stop attending to the actions we need to take in order to make our desired future possible. When we get caught in what-if thinking, we feel helpless and doomed, and as a result, disconnected from our present reality and our part in it. We've forgotten that how we behave today has everything to do with what tomorrow will bring, forgotten that we have agency and are part of the creation of our future. When we're catastrophizing, we're not only escaping from uncertainty, but we're also escaping from our current responsibilities. We are avoiding what we need to be focusing on to create the future we want.

What's particularly strange and baffling about this form of negative thinking is its utter senselessness. Life already contains enough catastrophes, real ones to live, without our having to think up any of our own. We don't need to create a disaster wait-list of potential horrors to keep us busy—life is chock-full of unforeseen and scary realities without any help from us.

It's true that we can't control what's to come, but we can certainly affect it with the actions we take today. And so, when my client Ramona falls into the trenches, into a future in which she's a homeless person with unsolvable debt, I ask her how much time she's spent studying for her boards that day and whether she thinks it's enough time. Catastrophic thinking is challenged by boots-on-the-ground, reality-based investigation.

Ask Yourself: *Am I doing everything I can right now to make the future I want possible? Have I left no stone unturned? What am I not focusing on—because I have determined it's a hopeless future?*

Maybe it's time to turn your attention to taking the steps you can take—now. All you can ever do is your part at this moment. Breaking free from excessive thinking means not only resisting the urge to create a story line about the future but also actively doing everything you can to create the outcome you desire. Pay attention to how you're behaving—now—and surrender the results. Read that sentence again.

Efforts to Be Prepared

Catastrophic thinking, furthermore, is a way to prepare ourselves for potential disasters. Our negative thinking loops, we imagine, help us stay fit so we're ready for hell when hell arrives. We think through every possible negative scenario to make sure we won't be surprised or ambushed by the future when it arrives. Catastrophic thinking is a misguided attempt to keep ourselves armed and ready.

Once again, however, we must inquire as to whether our mental preparations are actually helpful when it comes to handling negative outcomes if and when they do arrive. Does pre-living a disaster make us any better or more equipped to live it when it's here? In reality, the only thing we accomplish with our what-if thinking is to make sure that we get to experience the disaster at least once. With our what-if rehearsal, we know we won't have to miss out on the experience of disaster even if it never happens in real life. But in such preparations, we exhaust ourselves mentally and emotionally, deplete our nervous system, as we force our mind and body to run through the catastrophe that may never happen.

I've never heard a single person say, "Oh, I'm so glad I worried about this disaster ahead of time. Wow, that worrying is really helping me navigate this disaster now." So too, I've never come across a case when the catastrophe the person was replaying in their head was the same catastrophe that played out in real life. The disaster we imagine is never the exact shape or color of the one that comes, if one comes at all. Regardless, our preparations are for naught. We're always preparing for something different than what shows up.

Practice Probability

Catastrophic thoughts simultaneously hijack our present moment and hold us hostage with fear. When we catastrophize, we effectively take a fresh and unsuspecting now and blow it up with negative projections. Our projections may be about the future, but they are alive here, now. We're thinking about the disastrous future in this moment. Our fear-based, future-related thoughts poison the present moment and turn it into something that it isn't, something both dreadful and imaginary.

When we've convinced ourselves that something terrible is headed our way, usually, we've lost touch with probability. Probability is a simple but sturdy approach; it can serve as our life vest in the tsunami of catastrophic thinking.

Sarah and I had been working together for a long time, and I knew her inner hypochondriac well. Sarah spent a lot of time thinking about illness and had convinced herself on many occasions that she was suffering from one terminal condition or another. Any new sensation or physical change led her to frantically search the internet for an explanation. Soon after, she was convinced that she didn't have long to live. I had traversed this cycle with Sarah many times, and each time, she descended fully down the rabbit hole, getting her proverbial affairs in order. Sarah was extremely committed to and fully invested in her catastrophic thoughts. In her mind, the thoughts were not just thoughts, but cold hard reality.

During one of these trips down the rabbit hole, Sarah's mind was suffering with what she believed was a terminal autoimmune condition, a disease that was not only very rare but mostly found in people fifty-plus (she was in her thirties). I proposed the following: since we didn't know for sure that she was dying from this condition and since her symptoms could have been a result of a variety of possibilities, for now, was she willing to just go with probability? Until we had hard evidence that proved otherwise, could we give ourselves permission to assume what was statistically most likely? Remarkably, with this simple approach, Sarah was able to calm down and release her grip on her what-if thinking. Just for now, she was going to let the numbers win, let the probable be her reality.

Patty's catastrophic thoughts, on the other hand, had convinced her that her teenager was never going to get into college. She would be "lying on the couch watching TV for the rest of her life"…in Patty's living room. This mom was already trying to figure out how she would be able to vacation, without guilt, and leave her daughter behind "on the couch," already worrying about how she would figure out dating with her daughter's limp body forever present in the house.

I first asked Patty if she could just acknowledge that she was caught in a pretty fierce storm of what-if thinking—an unknown and uncertain future filled with certain disaster. I invited her to take a break from the story line and offer herself a bit of compassion for how difficult a place she was in at this moment. Not the difficulty of what she was imagining, but the difficulty of being trapped inside this what-if thinking loop. She could, and the tears came.

After a few minutes, I asked if she was also willing to consider the probability of this scenario. Not as determined by her current catastrophic mind, but rather by the statistics for what had happened before at her daughter's school. Had any of the students ever failed to get into any college? And if so, how many students? She told me that it had never happened. I asked if she agreed that the probability was low that her daughter would be the first person in the history of the school to get in nowhere. Again, she agreed. I then asked if there were colleges that accepted pretty much anyone regardless of grades. Another yes. Emboldened by our progression, I asked a final question: Was she willing to live in the probability that she and her daughter weren't that different from everyone else who had walked this path before her? Could she rest in what was (strongly) probable, at least until we received information that proved otherwise? She was on board, and within moments, the catastrophic thoughts melted out of her awareness.

Debra, on the other hand, suffered with a brand of catastrophic specialness, which served to support her what-if thinking. She had convinced herself that she would have some never-before-seen reaction to a drug that the doctor gave her following a minor surgery. Undoubtedly, her body would react to this well-proven medicine in a way that was different than the millions of people who had taken the drug over decades. When I asked her why she thought she was so different than everyone else, why she was so negatively special, she laughed. The idea that we are the cursed one, the despicable one, and yet the cursed and despicable one at the center of the universe—that what is true for us is so different from what is true for everyone else—is part of what keeps our *what-if* thoughts in power. We need to remind ourselves that we are not so unique and special when it comes to misfortune. If it's so for other human beings, chances are it's so for us as well.

When confronted with a situation that's unknown, we can actively choose to go with probability over our own distorted imagination, to hang on to history in the face of uncertainty, and to remember that we're not so different from everyone else.

Ask Yourself: *Is there a situation right now where I would benefit from considering the probability of what I'm imagining will happen, actually happening?*

If so, take a moment and lay out the external reality, with no story added on, as a replacement for the story inside your mind.

Just Get Through Now

Susan and her husband had decided they were going to divorce. It was a sad and stressful time: neither of them was happy about the decision, but as they saw it, there were no more options. With three young kids and shared property, a thousand things needed to happen to unravel this two-decade-long relationship. Their lives were intertwined in every way imaginable. Understandably, Sue was frightened and filled with anxiety and dread. Her entire life was going to change, and she knew it. Her thoughts, in trying to find something she could control in a situation that felt entirely out of control, were fixating on the most minute details. The decision to divorce wasn't a week old, but Sue's thoughts were frantically looping on which babysitters could take her daughter to school, how she would get the laundry basket up the stairs with her bad back, and where the air-conditioning switch was located so that in six months, when summer came, the house would be cool. Faced with the enormity of what was happening, Susan's mind grabbed onto the tasks that would have to be figured out later, but which couldn't possibly be figured out now.

When we can't stop thinking about all the things that will need to be figured out at some point in the future, it can be an act of supreme self-kindness to remind ourselves that we only have to and only can, in fact, manage the situation for today—just today. We cannot figure out what will be needed or wanted in the future. We don't have the information to decide that yet, so it's best to not go there until we know more. And, when we do go there, we don't have to do it alone. We can ask for help; other people have walked through whatever we're walking through, and we can call on those resources.

When we feel overwhelmed or scared, we need to give ourselves permission to stop figuring out the future and focus on today, to stop asking ourselves to know anything other than what's needed right now. We only have to get through this moment—now. We can say to ourselves, just for today: *Sweetheart...take this one day at a time.* This attitude and these sorts of words, offered with kindness and compassion, can grab us by the scruff of the neck and pull us straight out of the thinking hole of anxiety, fear, and despair.

Help the Imagined Scenario Reach Resolution

If we look closely, catastrophizing writes the future disaster script only to the point in the story when the catastrophe happens. Because we're hardwired to overestimate threats and underestimate our resources and abilities for dealing with them, we fail to write the part of the script that has us attending to the disaster itself. It can be useful, therefore, to write more, not less. That is, to keep going, playing the movie out in our head past the point where we normally run out of the theater in terror.

When you give yourself the chance to think about what you would do if the disastrous situation you're imagining were to happen, you can come up with some possible solutions or actions to take. Perhaps you may even have dealt with something similar in the past, if not in reality, then most probably in your head.

Ask Yourself: *Let's say this happens, then what? What would or could I do? What might be a next right step? Is there anyone I could ask for help? Have I ever faced something equally challenging in the past? If so, what helped me then?*

When we imagine what we would do if a catastrophe really did happen, sometimes we can't imagine anything at all. One of my clients keeps enough sleeping pills in her medicine cabinet to commit suicide if something terrible were to happen to her child. For her, the solution is that there isn't going to be an after-disaster to address. But it's important to recognize that the person we will be if that disaster happens is not the person who's sitting here now trying to imagine it or figure out a plan. The one who will be reacting to that challenging situation, if it happens, has not been created yet. We haven't yet been changed by the reality of that disaster. And so, if we can't imagine a way through, can't play the movie any further than the catastrophe, that's okay. You won't be then who you are now. That said, you can't know what will be possible or what will help get you through.

Vanessa had a dreadful fear of cancer. She was certain that if she ever did get a cancer diagnosis, she would emotionally collapse and die, not of the disease, but of fear. But when the time came that, unfortunately, she did receive the diagnosis, the Vanessa who walked through it and to its healthy conclusion was utterly different than the person she had imagined and unrecognizable from the person who had been fearing it. Life changes who we are. And often, a resilience and fortitude appear within us that we just can't imagine from the other side of reality, before they're needed.

EXERCISE: FINDING PROOF OF RESILIENCE

Recall a time from your past when you found your way through a situation that initially felt impossible or that you would have considered devastating.

1. Consider how you were able to navigate it or perhaps build a new relationship with the situation, either internally or externally.

2. Contemplate how that difficult situation changed you, what you learned from it, and how it changed your relationship with yourself and the world.

3. Take a moment to explore and acknowledge your own resilience and adaptability.

Catastrophic thinking is an attempt to take care of yourself by preparing you for impending doom. But in the process, you discount and dismiss who you really are: your strength and ingenuity, your life experience, your internal resources, and the support system you can tap if need be. If you don't believe me, look to your past for proof.

When you combine self-criticism, grievance, resentment, blame, fear, worry, anger, and righteousness, throw in a handful of catastrophic thinking, then shake it up in a mixer called life, you end up with a cocktail of suffering. Once we become aware of our negative thinking loops, what they're trying to accomplish, the imaginary assumptions and beliefs they're built on, the self-identities they support, and the damage they're causing in our lives, we can then choose a path. We can decide for ourselves what we want to engage in with regard to the thoughts our mind is throwing at us. Armed with awareness and self-compassion, we no longer have to bite the hook that our thoughts forever dangle or, for that matter, award them with a power they don't possess without our giving it to them.

PART II

Tools for Relief

CHAPTER 6

Unstick from Sticky Thoughts

Caulobacter crescentus, a bacterium that lives in water, holds the title for the stickiest substance on earth. It secretes a sugary compound three times stronger than superglue. A tiny bit of it can withstand the pull of lifting several cars at once.[12] As impressive as this sounds, if it were possible to compare the stickiness of *Caulobacter* to that of thoughts, I would still bet on thoughts as being the stickiest substance on earth.

You've probably noticed that certain thoughts are easier to let go of than others. Thoughts like, *What should I have for dinner? What's the weather going to be this weekend? What movie should I see?* aren't usually problematic in terms of shifting our attention elsewhere. There aren't strong emotions, history, or importance attached to these kinds of thoughts. Other kinds of thoughts, however, feel harder or downright impossible to escape. Thoughts connected to hurt, shame, resentment, anger, and other strong emotions, those tethered to our self-esteem and other strong beliefs…these are the kinds of thoughts that stick and stay stuck to us.

Sticky thoughts don't respond to our attempts to stop thinking them. No matter how we try to distract ourselves, scold ourselves for having them, assure ourselves they're not true, replace them with better thoughts, or any other strategy…they just won't let us go or let us let go of them. It can feel like the thoughts are literally superglued to our brain. These kinds of thoughts require a different approach. Fighting with them with more thoughts and other traditional methods won't work because their glue is stronger than any fight we can wage.

But as it turns out, we have a tool that we can use, one that can dissolve the glue that coats our thoughts. We can change the mind, our mind, to which the thoughts are adhering so the thoughts no can longer latch onto our attention with such ferocity. Awareness is that tool. When we become aware of just how sticky thoughts are, what beliefs empower their stickiness, and why we have so much trouble detaching from them, we are then able to dissolve the stickiness and smooth out the surface of our mind so the thoughts can peel away.

This chapter is devoted to the various aspects of ourselves—beliefs, ideas, and conditioning—that make us so receptive to the glue of thoughts. With this new awareness, the potential for freedom appears.

Believing Thoughts Are True

We stay stuck in thinking because of what we believe about our thoughts. Put simply, we believe *them*. We think our thoughts are trustworthy and true. By the very fact of their having appeared, they are deserving of our attention. We mistakenly believe our thoughts matter, regardless of what else we know that might contradict them or make them suspect. With this deep reverence for thoughts, it seems unwise to turn away from them. Why would we reject what we trust most?

The mind, maker of thoughts, convinces us that what it's telling us is…reality. And, consequently, that we can't live without its input and without accepting its authority. Thinking is the best thing we've got going for us (or so say our thoughts). In propagating this message, the mind cleverly secures itself as the necessary ingredient for our happiness and survival. We keep thinking excessively, not just because we believe our thoughts, but also because we are convinced that thinking is fundamentally good for us.

At the same time, we can't stop thinking because we don't realize we're thinking. We think without any awareness we're doing it. Thinking is always going on in the background and foreground of consciousness; it's the soundtrack to our life. To be thinking is to be alive. Thinking feels like just *being*. We don't know that silence and space can even exist between thoughts, that *we* can exist in the absence of thinking.

Furthermore, we don't know that thoughts can appear and we can choose to decline their invitation, decide not to engage in their content. We don't know another way of living, other than thinking.

Being in Love with Our Thoughts

We don't just trust and believe our thoughts, truth be told; we are utterly infatuated with thoughts. We find our own thoughts fascinating, delightful, visionary, and brilliant, and are utterly enamored with the contents of our mind. Our thoughts are what make us special; the better the thoughts, the better we are as the one who thought them up. The questions our thoughts raise are of utmost importance and value (to us) and must be answered, each one, with care and attention. When I asked a self-identified thinking addict what she thought it would be like to experience more gaps between her thoughts, spend less time thinking, she said it would be "like asking her to break up with a great lover." Indeed, many of us experience a kind of love affair with thoughts, attending to and valuing them above everything else in our life.

Breaking free from our addiction to thinking would mean breaking up with our greatest love, demoting our thoughts from our most favorite thing to something not so special, not so interesting, and possibly not even worthy of our attention.

Taking Ownership of Thoughts

It's odd, really, that we refer to the words we hear in our heads as *our* thoughts, as if they're something we come up with, make happen, and script. And yet, the words we hear, the substance of which we're taking credit or blame for, appear entirely without our consent, and without our crafting. Think about it: would you really choose most of the thoughts that appear in your consciousness? Thoughts appear whether we choose them or not and whether we sanction their appearance. So, in what way are they ours? Yes, we are the only ones hearing the thoughts but we certainly have not scripted them, agreed to them, or invited them into our consciousness. Our thoughts are not ours at all, not something we have chosen to create. Rather, they are random bits of content containing characters, emotions, and situations pulled from our life, popping up out of the soup of our own experience—usually for no particular reason.

Maintaining the Illusion of Control

We stay hooked into our thoughts because thinking gives us a sense of control. It makes us feel like we're doing something for ourselves, working on our own behalf. Thinking gives us a sense of agency, makes us feel less vulnerable and afraid, less at the mercy of change and what we can't control. We don't know another way, don't know how to let go of what we see as our lifeboat. We're so heavily invested and reliant upon thinking as the way to keep ourselves safe that we don't stop for long enough to get a glimpse of another way, a way of living that doesn't necessitate constant thinking.

We hold the deep conviction that thinking will make whatever we're thinking about better. It's ingrained in us from the time we're born: thinking is the solution—to every problem and nonproblem. But what if it's not? What if the premise at the center of everything we believe and do is faulty? What if thinking, the way we do it, is actually the problem, not the solution?

Assuming We Can Control Thought

No matter how out of control and random our thoughts may be, still, we believe that we should be able to control them and, somehow, make them reasonable. This belief, that thoughts are ours to control, contributes to our difficulty in letting them go. We imagine that if we really wanted to, tried hard enough, we would be able to stop unwanted thoughts from happening, to control our mind and create a life in which only wanted thoughts appeared. We are convinced that we have to keep fighting with thoughts until they go away and fighting with ourselves for not controlling them better. Ultimately, we can't leave our thoughts alone because we are responsible for their content and responsible for the fact that they're appearing.

Fearing Invasive Thoughts

Healthy, well-adjusted people can experience thoughts that just show up with no rhyme or reason, successfully scare and distract their recipient, and then disappear as randomly and senselessly as they appear. When Kevin is driving, a thought frequently appears in his mind that says, *You are going to swerve this car into someone on the side of the road.* Kevin is not homicidal but has heard this thought since he started driving thirty years ago. For Jane, an accomplished and experienced equestrian, the days leading up to each competition are peppered with thoughts telling her she is going to fall and break her neck and that these are the last days of walking and breathing on her own. Kimberly's invasive thought is she is going to jump into the subway tracks. She hears this thought almost every day on her commute to work, which leads her to look away from the train and hold onto a pole, just in case. Henry's unwanted thought tells him during theater performances that he is going to scream out and disrupt the performance. Essentially, the most inappropriate thing he can think of doing. This thought has been so bothersome and threatening that it caused him to give up seeing theater altogether.

While our invasive thoughts may be short-lived in their own right—momentary frightening whispers in the shadows of our mind—nonetheless, we put an enormous amount of time and energy into discounting and disproving them and trying to make them stop. We consider our thoughts to be far more important than just what they're yammering on about. Additionally, we think it's our responsibility to figure them out, decode their hidden meaning, understand why this particular thought is appearing now. We believe our thoughts hold some deep truth about who we really are, as if underneath it all, we secretly want to jump in the train tracks, scream out in a theater, or harbor an unconscious desire to be paralyzed. When such disruptive thoughts appear, it then becomes our responsibility to unearth what they're here to tell us.

Thoughts, as we imagine them, are a reflection of our unconscious drives and deepest longings, whispers from our soul. If thoughts say it, then it must be real, even if we don't know it yet. If we don't analyze and unravel our thoughts, we will be letting our true nature run amok, giving the green light to our deepest, darkest self. We have to get to the bottom of our thoughts so we can convince them they're wrong about us. If we don't, they will be right about us, and if not now, then soon.

At the same time, we think our thoughts have the power to make us do things entirely out of character, abhorrent even to our wishes, morals, and values. While we may have been a kind and decent person our whole life, the appearance of a violent thought makes us feel that deep down we must be a violent person, must want to commit violent acts, and are destined to do so. We give our thoughts the power to override everything we already know about ourselves. We imagine that our thoughts can compel us to act—without our consent. Thoughts are more powerful than us. We therefore have to aggressively refute our thoughts and prove beyond a shadow of a doubt that what they're suggesting will not happen. We have to do this again and again to ensure that the thoughts will not come true.[13]

But of course, we can't disprove such thoughts because we're operating in the land of, dare I say, crazy. We're in the company of a motherboard without an operator. There is no sense to the system or to these thoughts, yet we continue trying to use sense to disprove what's not real. The thoughts just happen. Why they happen is not a question that will help you recover from them.

What we resist persists. When we react to our thoughts as if they hold great importance, the power to make us do things we don't want to do, we turn them into something that matters. Our resistance gives our thoughts something to push against and in so doing, strengthens them. Our fear and resistance are their fuel. When we stop fretting about our disruptive thoughts, stop fearing them and trying to fight them off, stop investing them with the power to control us, and just accept them as a part of the out-of-order computer that is our mind, the very same disruptive thoughts, with the very same crazy content, cease to be so disruptive. The thoughts may still come (although usually far less often), but we know that we don't need to convince them or ourselves that they're wrong about us. Furthermore, we don't need to know why we don't want to do what they're telling us we want to do.

Our thoughts cannot make us do anything we don't want to do. Their appearance in no way suggests that we secretly want to do what they're proposing. Our thoughts aren't privy to any inside story on us. Invasive thoughts are just random firings from an out-of-order computer. Thoughts don't have to mean anything unless we choose to infuse them with meaning. We can actually leave our thoughts alone, allow them to hoot and holler, rant and spew, all the while knowing they cannot turn us into the crazy characters their content may suggest.

Fighting with our unwelcome thoughts, blaming ourselves for what's not in our control, doesn't change our thoughts. It does, however, keep us hooked in an unending cycle of thinking and paralysis. Thoughts keep coming, and we keep fearing and fighting with them. But fortunately, we are only responsible for how we respond to our thoughts. When we give up trying to make our thoughts stop, to change what the thoughts are telling us, we may lose the battle against our thoughts, but we will win the war with life. When we accept that thoughts just happen, that they're not our fault and not ours to control, this is victory. This is freedom—freedom *with* thoughts, not *from* thoughts. We can now get on with our life.

In the same way we might turn a deaf ear to a disturbed person on the street randomly yelling insane comments at us, we are wise to employ a similar attitude toward our invasive negative thoughts. We have com-passion for that mentally ill person, and yet, we don't pull up a chair and sit down with this shouter—to try to unpack and analyze the deeper meaning and purpose of their words, show them why they're not appro-priate, prove that they're not true. So too, we don't have to spend our energy discounting or plumbing our thoughts for deeper meaning. Their existence does not imply significance. We can simply acknowledge our inner intruder, our inner crazy, give her a name perhaps, recognize that she snuck her way into the control room. We nod to our crazy intruder… sigh, giggle, grimace, or whatever feels right…and just keep walking.

Once again, I repeat: we are not our thoughts. We are the awareness the thoughts are arising to and within. Most thoughts don't matter, and some thoughts really don't matter. Every moment we invest in our unwanted thoughts, every ounce of energy we put into trying to disprove them, is a morsel of time and energy wasted. We are validating and strengthening what's insignificant—a strange, albeit noisy blip in a flawed system.

Our thoughts, most importantly, offer us an opportunity to know ourselves more deeply. But not through their content, not by decoding their words (as we imagine). Rather, we come to know ourselves by deciding how we want to relate to our thoughts and, paradoxically, when we render thoughts irrelevant. Letting thoughts come and go without engaging with them or falling under their spell allows us to experience ourselves *as* the awareness within which the thoughts are appearing, the awareness that is deciding to let the thoughts go. When we separate from thoughts, we experience ourselves *as* the consciousness that hears the thoughts but is not made of them. We know ourselves, therefore, as who we really are.

Ignoring Deeper Causes

In psychology, there's an expression: "If it's hysterical, it's historical." If a situation is making you feel particularly emotional or out of control, it's probably related to something you lived at another time, when you were younger, and probably with your early caretakers. The same can be said for your thoughts: if it feels like you're stuck like glue to a set of thoughts, it's probably about something more than just what you're ruminating on, more than what it looks like on the surface.

You're stuck because you're trying to figure out or fix an experience from an earlier time in your life, to resolve feelings that were never resolved. You're in relationship with an old wound and a young self, which have been triggered by this current situation and which this thought loop is trying to work out. Once you understand this and stop buying into the story line the thoughts are spinning, and once you realize that your feelings are not just (and not really) about what your thoughts are telling you they're about, you can then loosen your grip on the situation at hand and ease up on urgently having to solve it. In so doing, you are not only freeing yourself from the particular thoughts you're locked up in, but you're also breaking the addictive thinking patterns that keep you mentally hooked into every new problem that arises.

The next time you're caught in a sticky thought loop, obsessing and replaying a situation, when you feel like you positively must figure it out or you can't be happy, stop and ask yourself, *What is the felt experience that this situation triggers in me? Am I feeling not heard, not seen, not loved, blamed? Do I feel like I have no voice or no way to protect myself? What can I not make happen? What is the core experience for me in this situation?* Once you get a sense of the core experience, continue by asking yourself, *Have I ever felt this feeling before? If so, with whom, and how?* I would also recommend journaling on these questions. What's important is that you get in the habit of contemplating and reflecting on the deeper thread lines behind your thought loops, which will help loosen your attachment to the situation at hand and what looks like is in the way of your being okay.

Once you identify, reflect, and maybe write on the core experience, take a moment to offer yourself some kind words. Place a hand on your heart and remind yourself that what you're experiencing right now matters; tell yourself, *This matters.* If you feel unheard, you can say to yourself, *I hear you; I care about what you're experiencing; I get it.* If you're feeling unloved, you can tell yourself, *I love you right here, just as you are.* Whatever words soothe the core experience, offer them to yourself. Use this new awareness of the core wound under the sticky thinking as an invitation, above all else, to be fiercely self-loving.

Replacing Life with Ideas About It

When I was a little girl, I believed that a flower *was* a flower—that this thing I called a flower contained some fundamental essence of flower-ness. Why else would we call it a flower? Later, on a family trip to Holland, I discovered that Dutch people called this thing I knew to be a flower a *bloem*, and later when we arrived in Spain, the same thing became a *flor*. I was thoroughly confused. "But it's a flower, so why do they call it *bloem* or *flor*? Why don't they just call it what it is?" I asked my father, not comprehending that the word "flower" was not the same thing as this extravagantly colored, deliciously smelling entity I so enjoyed.

From the time we develop language, we start experiencing life through words and then later ideas and concepts. Once we learn the word "flower," then when we see something that looks like a flower, we immediately think, *Oh, that's a flower*, with the implication that we already know what this thing is that we're looking at. Once we attach the label to it, we categorize and conceptualize not just the object, but also the whole experience that is a flower. We assume we already know what it is, and so we stop really looking at it—stop seeing its color, smelling its scent, feeling its texture, noticing its uniqueness, stop actually experiencing it. We see the object and immediately move into our ideas about flowers—all the information we ever learned about flowers and everything we associate with them, from our first Valentine's Day rose to the flowers we laid on our grandmother's coffin. There's no longer a need, desire, or even awareness of interacting with the flower directly. We have filed it away in our mind's cabinet of ideas and are now in a relationship with the concept of flower, rather than the flower itself. The lived experience of that flower has been replaced by the idea of it.

As we accumulate more language, ideas, and strategies for thinking about life, the distinction between our experience and the words that describe it shrinks and eventually disappears. We start to believe that our thoughts contain the essence of the experience they're describing, interpreting, opining on, and conceptualizing. The thoughts about our experience become synonymous with the experience itself. The stand-in becomes the actor. Just as I, as a young person, believed that the word "flower" was the same thing as a flower, so too, we believe our thoughts about life *are* life.

The longer we live, the less we remember what it's like or that it's even possible to experience life directly, without all our thoughts and concepts in the way. We get comfortable interacting with life through the layer (and lens) of thought...interacting, that is, with the packaging of life. Until ultimately, we forget what we're giving up, forget what's inside the packaging. We lose touch with the direct, sensorial experience of being alive—forget that life, raw and uninterpreted, still exists. The flower, while perhaps describable and intellectually knowable, is still an ever-changing and, to some degree, incomprehensible or unknowable experience. The result is that we live at arm's length from our experience, from our life, waylaid in the shallows of description and interpretation. Life becomes an abstraction—an intellectual quagmire. But rarely, if ever, do we swim directly in the depths of life, stripped naked of our wet suit of ideas.

It bears repeating: our thoughts about life are not life, but rather just descriptions, interpretations, abstractions, analyses, opinions, and everything else—about life. Our thoughts do not contain the experience of the thing they're talking about. While our thoughts may make a lot of sense, help us get things done, frame and direct life in useful ways, still, our thoughts are just mental constructions, replacements for our experience, which ultimately cannot be captured or lived fully through thought. Directly experiencing a flower through our senses, being awed by it, is not the same as thinking about what kind of flower it is or what season it blooms in, and not the same as deliberating on the fact that we enjoy this flower or considering who we're going to give it to, or anything else about it for that matter.

We start removing the layers of thought between us and life when we're ready...when we're courageous enough to stop turning every experience into a conceptual conundrum and curious enough to see what's here when there's nothing to have to explain or know about it. It happens, ultimately, when we're willing to stop thinking every moment into an idea of itself.

We hold tight to our thoughts about life because we don't trust or even know that life can be experienced in any way other than through thoughts and through the me who is thinking them. But life can indeed be met directly, without all the layers of thought between us and it.

We imagine that we are living a life—*our* life—as if life and *who we are* exist as two separate entities. But in fact, there is only one thing: we are inseparable from this thing we call life; we ourselves are life, part of its river. Consider for a moment: What if you are part of life rather than the one living it? What if there's no separate you and it? What if what you consider *you*, that is, all your thoughts and sensations, is also something arising in the larger consciousness? Feel what this contemplation stirs in your body. Walk with it, live with it.

Avoiding Existential Withdrawal

When you ask an addict if he can imagine life without his substance, he'll tell you absolutely, positively…never. Life without a fix is unfathomable. Reality, without a way out of it, without a way to create a different state of consciousness, would not be possible. An escape from reality is what an addict needs to survive reality. Similarly, if I asked you if you could imagine a life in which thinking were optional or in which moments of no thinking could even happen, you would probably tell me that such a thought is unthinkable. We're open to thinking about not thinking or thinking about how to control thinking (we love a good thought to chew on), but not thinking for real doesn't seem possible or even desirable. Not thinking is most definitely not a viable solution to the problem of thinking. And in fact, when we try to change our relationship with thought, reconsider the place of thinking in our life, our thoughts push back with their own brand of existential withdrawal.

"I think, therefore I am," surmised the seventeenth-century philosopher René Descartes. And indeed, we feel a sense of ourselves, a sense of being alive when we're thinking, solving a problem, or any other mental activity. We know ourselves through the act of thinking; we are the ones doing it, after all. Every now and again, however (and more frequently if you have a meditation practice), you might notice a gap between thoughts, a space of quiet in your mind, a moment when you were not thinking. When we notice these gaps, notice not thinking, often, we experience a kind of primal fear. The mind, realizing that it had momentarily stopped thinking, tends to panic. Our mind feels as if we disappeared and temporarily ceased to exist. When we stop thinking, we stop feeling our own presence in the way we're used to experiencing it. We stop experiencing ourselves as existing.

Gaps between thoughts can be experienced as annihilation, but in fact, they are the doorways to our freedom, glimpses of another way of being, and the kryptonite to our thinking addiction. When we discover that we still exist even when we're not thinking and that our own presence remains in the spaces between thoughts, then we can start to get more comfortable and curious in the gaps. Then we can break our reliance upon thinking as the only way to feel we actually exist.

EXERCISE: WHO'S HERE NOW?

Take a deep, slow breath. Relax. Tune into your senses. Feel the sense of just being. Notice what's here that doesn't rely on and isn't made of thought. Notice the presence that you don't have to think into existence. Contemplate: *Who's here now?*

Interestingly, while we're in the actual experience of not thinking, we're not afraid. There's no thought of fear, no thought of a *me* that's missing. The self does not miss itself when we're not thinking. In these moments, you could say there's no self to be afraid. In the flow experience, when we're deeply engaged in a sport or creative activity, the one who's doing it disappears, the thoughts about what's happening fade away. We are absorbed fully into the experience itself. Life becomes something we're inside of, rather than something a separate *I* is making happen. The experience of linear time disappears, and we're swallowed up into now. Without thought, we are no longer separate from our experience, no longer separated from life.

The instant we realize that we were not actively thinking, not here in the sense we normally experience ourselves—through our thoughts, that is—those same thoughts explode. Our mind screams, *What just happened? Where did I go? What does this say about me? What should I do about it? I've got to tell so-and-so about this…*and a thousand other thoughts about that moment when we were not thinking, not there. When we become aware of the gap, the space of being without thinking, we react by doubling down on thinking. We correct the existential terror that arises from having the idea of ourselves momentarily disappear from our consciousness. The sense of self-absence is thus replaced with a tsunami of thoughts, which then return us to a comfortable sense of ourselves, the one we know, the experience of ourselves that we achieve through the act of thinking. Back is the one thinking about not thinking.

What's clear is that the thought of not thinking—to the mind, maker of thoughts—is anything but desirable. Our mind is not keen on less thinking, on getting comfortable without thought. The mind is positively not in favor of a self that's independent from thoughts. Asking the mind if it wants to drop out of thought is like asking a fisherman if he wants to move to the desert. "No," he says, "what would I do there?" Asking our thinking self to get comfortable without thought is like asking a raindrop to join and thus disappear into the ocean. "No," says the raindrop, "I want to remain a unique, separate, and knowable raindrop self; I want to remain as me, the raindrop!" Not thinking, even temporarily, is tantamount to not existing. But it's precisely this thought that keeps us obsessively thinking. The next step, then, is to realize that you are bigger than thought.

CHAPTER 7

Discover the You That's Bigger Than Thought

People often ask me if it's possible, really possible, to recover from an addiction to thinking. The answer, without question, is yes—it's possible. But (and it's a serious but), in order to recover, we have to be ready to fall out of love with our thoughts and with our thinking process. We have to be willing to build a new kind of relationship with our thoughts, one in which who we are is separate from what our mind is telling us.

So too, to break any addiction, we have to hit bottom—our bottom, which may not be the same as anyone else's bottom. We have to be sick and tired of being sick and tired, anxious, worried, stressed, unhappy, and all the rest. We have to get fed up with our old thinking patterns and behavior, and the consequences they're creating. We have to get fed up enough to be willing to forge a new path—a new way of responding to our thoughts when they arise and a new way of thinking about thinking. There's one thing we can count on: if we keep doing what we've always done, we'll keep getting what we've always gotten. We need to take steps on a new path to go somewhere different. This chapter shares a journey to a fresh way of being.

Gain Distance with Inner Listening

The first step in breaking free from excessive thinking is making a commitment to listen in on our own mind—pay attention to our own consciousness. When we're caught in a thought loop of any kind, what we've lost is space…the space between the one listening to the thoughts and the thoughts themselves. We are fused with the thoughts and thus unable to hear or see them as distinct entities appearing in front of us. When we're caught, our thoughts don't appear as separate from who we are. Thoughts are us, and we are thoughts.

Through the practice of inner listening, listening to our own thoughts (without believing them), we start to create that space between us and our thoughts. By observing the words our mind is speaking to us, we are actively separating from our thoughts, getting them out in front of us, into view—creating an *us* and an *it*. In so doing, we're shifting our perspective so we are now the awareness that sees the thoughts, while the thoughts become objects appearing in front of and within us.

Inner listening is not only the practice of noticing thoughts, however. It is also the practice of paying attention to our own attention, noticing where our attention is tracking at any given moment, what it's following, and also what it wants to follow. As we get more skilled, we start seeing not just the thoughts appearing, but also how our own attention is leaning and pulling. The more we practice, the more subtle and refined our ability to notice becomes. Our awareness expands, and with it, our freedom.

EXERCISE: REDIRECT YOUR ATTENTION

Pause and notice the thoughts appearing in your consciousness. Notice what you're paying attention to. Now purposefully shift your attention away from where it wants to be. Feel what it's like to redirect your attention. Now shift your attention back to where it wants to be. Practice moving your attention around. Get a feel for that energy or intelligence that actually moves your attention. Take little moments throughout your day to step back and notice where your attention is attending. Play with it; move it around. Notice where your attention wants to go. Make paying attention to attention a regular practice. Continually invite the question, *Where is my attention right now?*

Inner listening is about becoming intimate with our own mind: expert in its tricks, tactics, and propaganda, aware of the ways our mind speaks and moves. The more attuned we are to our mind, the more we are able to hear our thoughts as they're arising, when they're still beckoning for our attention, but before we've disappeared into their lair. This gives us choices—a *say* in what kind of inner experience we are creating.

Our thoughts talk to us in our own voice, which makes it that much harder to see or hear them as something separate from us. Our negative thoughts use our beliefs, fears, past experiences, and everything else to make their case. Our thoughts sound like us, think like us, opine like us, and feel like us...and yet (thankfully) they are not us. In this case, they walk, talk, and quack like ducks, but they are not ducks!

In order to see our thoughts as separate from who we are, we have to build the habit of listening closely and consistently to the activity and noise that's taking place in our own head, without believing or indulging it. We have to cultivate the skill and habit to turn our ear inward and tune in to our mind's radio station, the one we're listening to even if we don't know we're listening, even if the volume is turned way down. Listening inward is the primary practice for unhooking from negative thinking, the one we can't do without—the one practice that is a requirement for freedom.

Disentangle with Acknowledgment and Acceptance

As soon as we become aware of negative, obsessive, or any kind of excessive thought, we have to first stop, step off the hamster wheel, and acknowledge the fact that the thoughts are coming and that we're caught in them. We simply mark the present reality of being flooded, deluged, attacked, consumed, or whatever else applies—by our thoughts. We stop and say, *Wow, I'm really caught*, or *My mind is really hammering me*, or whatever acknowledgment feels right in that moment. In so doing, we are deliberately taking some distance from those thoughts, distinguishing ourselves as the one who's hearing them, but is *not* defined by them. We are setting up two entities, an *us* (awareness) and a *them* (thoughts).

The moment we recognize what's happening in our mind is the moment we start to feel relief. Acknowledging the presence of thoughts, ironically, allows us to feel disentangled from the thoughts and the whole thinking storm. With acknowledgment, suddenly, there's a safe and separate shore from which to observe the thoughts without being drowned by them.

It can also be helpful in this acknowledgment and acceptance stage to give a name to our negative thinker. When we label this voice of negativity inside us, it lightens and separates us from the negative messages. Naming creates space. We can use a few different names too: Matilda for our catastrophizer, the one who reminds us of everything that could (and will) go wrong; Barbara for our self-critic, the one who reminds us of everything wrong with us; Hal for our grievance keeper, the one who reminds us of every injustice anyone has ever done to us. If you like, match the kind of thoughts to the names of people you've known who remind you of such sentiments, then have at it. What's key is that when the thoughts arise, we take a moment to acknowledge the voice with its proper name, *Oh look, it's Matilda…here to tell me that I'm going to fail and that it will all end poorly. Thank you for sharing, Matilda! Now you can go!*

Offer Yourself Compassion

When we recognize that the negative thoughts are here, we need to pause and name this truth as well. We need to take a moment to consciously offer ourselves a dose of compassion, here, at the center of the storm. We can place one hand on our heart, take a breath, and simply say, *This matters, my experience matters.* There is nothing more important in the healing process than to remind ourselves of the most basic and loving truth of all—our suffering matters. We matter. Knowing (which sometimes means learning) this truth is at the root of all transformation.

If more kindness is wanted or needed, we might also say something like, *Wow, I'm really trapped,* or *This is really painful,* or *I really wish this would stop.* Whatever the words that come, we take a moment to honor our experience—what it's like right here where we are. This compassionate pause, the acknowledgment of our own experience, is a critical and unskippable step in the process of breaking free from our self-inflicted unkindness.

Inner listening, recognition, acknowledgment, and compassion are the roots of recovery and, in this case, recovery from our addiction to thinking. These fundamental processes lay the ground for transformation. Once we've recognized the truth of what's happening in our mind, acknowledged what we're doing to ourselves, and offered ourselves compassion for our own experience, we can then play with a variety of different contemplations and practices.

Get Curious About Your Own Mind

A warning: If, after hearing and acknowledging your thoughts, you start fighting with them again or trying to change them, prove them wrong, or annihilate them, you will once again begin working on behalf of your negative thoughts, re-energizing them. The time and attention you invest in fighting with your thoughts actually strengthens them and helps them to better mount their attack. What we resist persists and persists with a vengeance, fueled by our own fighting energy. So, knowing this, remind yourself to do what's most unnatural, that is, give up the fight against what feels most dangerous and instead of fighting, get really curious about your own mind.

Here are some questions that you can pose in the moment, shared as stories so you can perceive their power at work.

What Am I Believing Right Now?

Cara was taking a walk with her closest childhood friend. They were laughing and enjoying each other's company. Her friend jokingly said that he didn't make friends easily, to which she sweetly and playfully replied, "Well, you made friends with me." His response was, to her ears, a lukewarm, unenthusiastic, and even disappointed, "Uh huh." She was not happy. They had been having a lovely time, and in an instant, she was hurt and angry and turned around and headed home.

As she walked, a tornado was building inside her head at the center of which was the thought that her best friend had just taken a sweet moment, a moment of connection, and intentionally thrown it away. Her thoughts had also decided that he didn't think it was so great that he had made friends with her back in middle school and would actually rather have other friends than her. With each step, she was becoming angrier, more resentful, more hurt, and more convinced of her story line.

Back at home, it suddenly dawned on her to ask herself the following question: Was the choice she was making in that moment—to stick with her story about what had just happened—moving her closer to happiness or unhappiness? The answer was easy. She knew beyond a shadow of a doubt that if she stuck with what she was thinking, her evening and maybe even her next couple of days would be prickly, tense, and awful. She wondered if it was really worth it when she could make a different choice and change the whole trajectory of her next thirty-six hours and beyond.

But the question she asked next was the one that really snapped her out of her story and ultimately propelled her to take a different action. She asked herself if she actually believed her own story. Did she believe that the meaning she was assigning to this interaction was really true?

With these questions posed, she realized that she was thinking herself into a miserable lather about something she herself didn't even believe was true. She didn't believe her friend wanted or intended to hurt her or that he wished he were friends with other people instead of her. This new awareness then allowed her to see the ridiculousness in continuing to invest in her current thoughts and continuing to react to them as if they were true. It also allowed her to feel an entirely different feeling toward her friend. Realizing that he did not want to hurt her actually made her appreciate his kindness—appreciate him.

What Would I Need to Know?

Sarah, on the other hand, had just come out of a big fight with her husband. She was as mad as a wet hornet. She went through the same loop, about how he didn't listen, didn't remember anything she ever told him, and became defensive when she expressed frustration about constantly having to repeat herself. After listening to her replay the same mental tape for the umpteenth time, I asked Sarah what she would need to know, what she *could* know, that would allow her to let go of this narrative. What truth or understanding (other than her husband learning to pay attention) would free her from this thought loop, would allow her to stop replaying her grievances and reliving her pain? We sat in silence for a minute. When she did speak, what she said surprised me, and her too. Even more surprising was that just realizing what she *needed* to know allowed her to know it…without any additional confirmation.

Sarah uncovered two things. First, she discovered that if she could know that she fundamentally did not need her husband, did not need him to be happy or even okay, then this truth would free her from having to keep engaging in this particular grievance loop. If she could know that she would be okay with or without him, then her husband could continue forgetting what she told him, or not, but her basic well-being would not be dependent upon his changing. She could then feel at peace and free from the need to control or change him. Armed with the knowing of what she needed to know (to be okay), Sarah was able to start offering herself this truth, which deep down she already knew, but along the way had lost sight of. She told herself the exact words she needed to hear: *I will be okay, no matter what, with or without him.* She said these words out loud, which allowed her to start focusing on her own happiness and drop out of this fight in her mind and with her husband.

Through asking this question, she realized something else important too. She discovered that if she didn't have to explain to her husband why his behavior was upsetting and if it wasn't her responsibility to get him to agree with and empathize with her, then she would be able to leave this thinking pattern in the dust. Then, she would be free from having to keep rehashing her rightness and confirming the legitimacy of her resentment. Furthermore, if she could know that her husband didn't have to understand her feelings in order for her to get to have them, then she would be okay. Then the struggle in her head would be over.

As it turned out, amazingly, just by getting clear on what she needed to know—the *if this were true*—Sarah discovered that she already knew it. In her gut, Sara knew that her feelings did not require her husband's understanding or validation in order to exist, that her experience was real, valid, and deserving of kindness on its own, without any explanation or defense. But, she also saw how she had been believing she had to come up with a way of explaining her feelings that her husband could understand and that it wasn't until he *got it* that she would be validated and thus relieved. It wasn't until *he* allowed her feelings a seat at *his* table that she could be okay. But Sarah was able to go beyond these thoughts and beliefs by directly accessing and holding her own experience—without having to describe and explain them. As a result, Sarah broke free from the painful and obsessive thinking about *why* she was upset and *why* she was entitled to empathy. Just by knowing what she needed to know, she discovered what she already knew—a discovery that gave her the kindness and understanding she sought.

It is an act of self-compassion just to ask ourselves the question, *What would I need to know that would free me to let go of these thoughts? If I could know this, I could move on.* The next time you get caught in a negative thought loop, consider this inquiry. I call this question an act of self-compassion because even before we get to an answer, the question invites us into a space inside ourselves that holds what we know at a gut level but haven't yet formulated or allowed ourselves to know or feel. The place where we go looking for an answer to this question is the place of our heart's longing, where we carry our real hurts, intuition, and also, real wisdom. The asking and discovering itself is an act of kindness—a recognition of the longing and truth within us that rarely receives our full attention. If we ask our head this question, *What would free us to move on?* we will get a series of answers that may all be true, but don't usually touch the real pain we're carrying. As well, they're usually answers we already know, a list of our well-established grievances newly framed as if already resolved. When we pose this question to our heart and gut, however, and pause to really listen, we tend to find a more meaningful response and a response that, in and of itself, helps us move forward.

Offer Yourself What You Need Most

Once we uncover what we wish we could know, we can then offer ourselves the morsels of comfort and wisdom we crave. And here's the thing: we can do this even if it doesn't feel 100 percent certain or true—yet. Just the act of offering ourselves the words we need to hear, spoken inside or aloud, is comforting and calming and filled with self-compassion. We might say to ourselves, "You're going to be okay no matter what happens," or "I love you, and you're good—no matter how this plays out," or "You can be happy even if nothing about this situation ever changes." The point is to give yourself (and receive) the words of love and support that hit your sweet spot, bring your particular wounds relief and comfort, and set you free. If you're willing to use it, this question and offering can be a powerful tool in shutting off excessive thinking.

Face Your Fear of Letting Go

When we're caught in a repetitive thought loop, it can feel like we literally have no choice but to continue spinning around in the same tornado until the thoughts decide to free us. But sometimes, it can feel like we ourselves are choosing to stay looped in, spinning in the cyclone, despite how awful it feels. Sometimes, when we try to extricate ourselves from a particular line of thinking, the urgency to stay with it, to keep the loop looping, can feel like a matter of life and death...as if turning away from the thoughts would risk our very survival. Letting go of the thoughts, it seems, would be far worse than staying in the thoughts. In such cases, we can actually use the intensity as an opportunity to become more self-aware. We can ask ourselves: *If I drop these thoughts and move on, what am*

I afraid will be lost? What hope or possibility will be threatened? What part of me will die?

It's often the case that our repetitive thought loops, particularly the life-and-death sort, are trying to preserve or support a certain self-image or identity. The belief is this: if we can get the other person to perceive us in the way we want to be perceived, see us as the person we want to be seen as, then (and only then) we will get to experience ourselves as that kind of person—will get to *be* that person. We can't stop thinking about how we're going to correct or control the other person's perception of us because our own identity depends upon it.

The drive to be perceived and experienced in a certain way gives birth to much of our addictive thinking. And, it is this sort of thinking that can feel particularly sticky and impossible to leave behind. If we were to stop obsessing on the preservation and protection of our own identity, we would then risk the other's version of us, their story about us, becoming the one that defines us, the one that's considered true. To let go would mean to give up on being seen as who we want to be seen as and, sometimes, give up on getting to experience ourselves as that because the two are linked. Further, what would perish would be the opportunity to be seen and known for who we *really* are, our goodness, and the very best in us. Abandoning such a thinking loop is tantamount to allowing the good version of ourselves to die. It all sounds a bit strange and nebulous, but inside the mind, these kinds of life-and-death battles are going on all the time.

Just Say No!

We repeat the same negative thoughts to ourselves again and again, so why not repeat the same helpful thoughts with equal ferocity and redundancy? And indeed, here's one to repeat: *No!* No, I will not listen to, will not believe, will not attend to, will not respect, and will not indulge in this negativity against myself. The most powerful weapon we possess in our arsenal against negative thoughts may be the simplest. This clear, direct, and no-nonsense thought (and instruction) is probably more effective and forceful than any sophisticated strategy ever invented. Regardless of what's happening in your mind, what thoughts are popping into consciousness, you, the one listening or not listening to those thoughts, are emboldened with the final veto power. Though you may never have known this truth or practiced it, you can actually say, *No. Stop it. Go away. Enough!* to the contents of your own thoughts.

You can also set up a mantra that contains a simple but definitive blanket order of self-protection to use whenever the urge to self-attack arises. Depending on your particular form of negative self-attack, it might be one of the following: *No! I will not shame myself, I will not blame myself, I will not criticize myself, I will not make fun of myself, I will not terrify myself, I will not devalue myself, I will not say mean things to myself. No...and no matter what!*

When we join the *no matter what* club, we get to use this mantra indiscriminately. We don't have to vet the thoughts coming down the pike, argue with them, mount a case against them, or prove they're wrong in order to pull out our *No* card. When we really take on this affirmation, with conviction, the reward is that we get to use this sweeping *No (I will not)* card without any justification whatsoever. If a thought has even a whiff of unkindness, we get to play our *No* card and leave it at that. What's amazing is that you can make the decision to join the *no matter what* club right now.

Inquire: "Can I Change This?"

There is yet another inquiry we can pull out of the toolshed. The inquiry is targeted at a primary source of excessive thinking, namely, our fierce and persistent need to be in control. We ask ourselves: *Do I have control over this situation I'm trying to control (through my thoughts)? Is it in my power to change this situation? How long have I been trying to change it, and has it worked so far?* We want to look deeply into the question of whether or not we are really in control. These questions (asked with curiosity, not criticism or mockery) can help us recognize those situations in which we really don't have control over the outcome, no matter how much we try to think the situation or person into what we want. Sometimes we have to fail long and hard enough, fail to change what we want to change, in order to realize that the situation is not ours to control. But when we get it, get that we're really not in charge, we also understand the absurdity and futility in our obsessive thinking.

Realizing what we cannot control marks the dawning of liberation. Realizing that we cannot change what we want to change, paradoxically, sets us free. We are no longer shackled to the problem and no longer responsible for making it something else. We can't make it different, and sometimes that's the best news we can receive.

No matter what we believe about God or a larger intelligence in the universe, even if we believe nothing of the sort, we can still benefit from invoking the serenity prayer. Indeed, when we pray for serenity, we don't have to be praying *to* anything. If we want to address the prayer to a God or higher power, we can, but it's not necessary for reaping the benefits in such an authentic plea. It goes like this: *Grant me the serenity to accept the things I cannot change, the courage to change the things I can, and the wisdom to know the difference.* We can offer ourselves this prayer at any moment and whenever we catch ourselves trying to think our way into controlling what's not ours to control. This simple prayer, this wish for ourselves—to accept what we cannot change and cannot control—is at the heart of our freedom from excessive thinking and from suffering.

Ask Whether You're Willing to Do Something Different

At the core of every change process lies the fundamental question: *Am I willing to do it differently? Am I willing to change?* If we cannot say yes to this question, then we're not ready to change, not ready to be free just yet. Ask yourself, "Are you ready—really ready to change—no matter what it takes?" It's okay if you're not; it's okay if right now you're just curious.

There's no right or wrong answer to this question. But it's important to get honest about where you are in the change process.

When it comes to our addiction to thinking, doing something different, at the very least, means being willing to release our grip on thoughts at precisely the moments we don't want to release our grip, when we think it would be most unwise to do so. And indeed, these are the moments we must be willing to do so—to try something new, even if we don't yet trust it. To try something new just because the way we're doing it is not working. As well, change means being willing to stop figuring out what we're convinced needs figuring out and to leave things un-figured out, unsolved, as they are.

Transformation, when it comes to our thinking, requires the willingness to consider that there might be another path to happiness, to peace—other than through more thinking. There might be a way we can't yet see and won't see, as long as we're relying on thinking to find it. Ultimately, we must be willing to consider the possibility that thinking is not the solution to life and might, in fact, be the problem itself.

The radical and radically different choice has to happen right inside the hurricane of thoughts. That is, the choice to let go of our thoughts, let go of the stories, again and again, and intentionally escort our attention back to the present moment. This is what we do differently. What changes then, through this process, is who we think we are—from the thoughts themselves to the one letting go of the thoughts. This is the fresh path we must be willing to walk, the change we must be willing to implement.

As you start observing your own mind and its particular patterns and styles, this new reality of *not* being your thoughts will find its own unique expression within you. What's important is that you pay close attention to what *relating with your thoughts differently* means for you and what change is necessary in your own process and habits. Practice what I offer here, but don't ignore your own inner wisdom. Listen inside. The goal here is to unlock a deeper awareness, one that knows itself as *not* thought and also knows freedom. This awareness can return you to the present moment and to the life that thoughts have kidnapped you from and from you.

CHAPTER 8

Come Back to the Life You're Missing

Excessive thinking takes us into some dark and dangerous neighborhoods inside our own mind. That much is clear. But thinking is also a thief. Thinking kidnaps the present moment and in so doing, kidnaps our life.

If we're busy thinking, we're not here. Our attention is somewhere else, which means we are somewhere else. Psychologists at Harvard discovered that we're lost in thought almost 50 percent of the time. For literally half our life, we're distracted and absent from what's happening in our present moment.[14]

Your Body Is Forever Present

When we imagine where our inner thinker is located, where the me that's doing the thinking actually lives in our physical body, most of us imagine it to be sitting somewhere behind our eyes or inside our head. We experience this entity we call me, the one thinking, as a miniature version of ourselves, a mini-me who sits inside our skull.[15]

When we're thinking, which is generally whenever we're awake, our attention and energy are focused inside our head, hence the expression "living in our head." As a result of our head-centered existence, we lose connection with our physical body. We forget that there's actually an organism transporting this head around, a whole universe below our neck. We end up walking around as little floating heads, clouds of thoughts, untethered from our physical reality.

Remarkably, no matter how much we're living in our head, our body is still here, still busy doing its thing, keeping us alive. Our body is here in the present moment regardless of whether our attention chooses to synch up with it. While our thoughts transport us out of now, to the past or future or into a movie in our mind, our body is attending to what needs to happen now.

In every moment, including this one, our body is breathing us, digesting the contents of our intestines, filtering the blood through our liver, signaling our heart to beat, and performing an infinite number of other life functions. Our body doesn't have the luxury of checking out or being distracted. If the body leaves now, that means we leave now, for good. Amazingly, the human being has been created with an innate and profound wisdom. The tasks associated with our survival have been assigned to something other than our mind. Anyone who's ever tried to meditate knows how hard it can be to keep our attention focused on a single breath, much less ten breaths in a row. Imagine what would happen if we had to rely on our attention to keep our heart beating or accomplish any of the other tasks our body does to keep us alive. The fact that we don't have to pay attention to staying alive in order to stay alive is great news. For one thing, it means that we'll get to stick around for a while, but it also means that we're provided, free of charge, with an amazing gift. Just south of our head sits a foolproof portal through which we can enter this present moment. The instant we drop into our senses, we've caught a direct flight into now.

EXERCISE: OUT OF YOUR HEAD, INTO YOUR BODY

Consciously shift your attention out of your head and down into your body. Unhook from your thought stream. Take a deep breath. Feel the weight and presence of your body, the inner hum of your own aliveness. Feel the experience of being embodied—fully here.

Explore what this feels like, inhabiting your body. Being, not doing. Know too that you can drop into this place of inner presence, of embodied being, whenever you wish or need. Forever present, your body waits for you to rejoin it.

Learn to Directly Experience Feelings

In addition to checking out of the body, thinking allows us to check out on our feelings—to avoid them. When we don't want to experience what we're living, even if we don't know exactly what it is, we use thinking as a way to escape. We are well trained and highly skilled at thinking about our problems; we know how to turn them around, upside down, and every which way—for hours, days, weeks, and even lifetimes. But we're often unskilled at actually feeling our feelings. We're afraid of difficult feelings and certain that if we do allow ourselves to feel our feelings, we'll be stuck in them forever. In response to the threat of emotional discomfort, the mind steers us in more familiar and safe directions. We get busy thinking about our problems: interpreting them, unpacking them, and devising solutions and strategies to solve them, all in a masked effort to avoid actually experiencing them. The mind will always choose to think about difficult emotions rather than feel them. Thinking is the most effective and universally accepted method we've got for avoiding our own experience.

Amazingly, we're never taught how to experience feelings, not directly anyway. Most people don't even realize that thinking about emotions is not the same thing as feeling them. From an early age, we learn how to make pro and con lists, to investigate and contemplate the causes of our feelings, to understand why we're feeling the way we are, and most of all to figure out a solution to the problems causing our feelings. But these mental gymnastics, while interesting and sometimes helpful for understanding and framing our experience, also keep us far away from the actual feelings themselves. We love the why questions: Why do we feel the way we do?—but we run from the what questions: What do we actually feel? And we run even faster from the possibility of actually feeling it.

Thinking and talking about our problems, while designed to keep us away from our feelings, actually leave us stuck in them. In fact, the only way through a difficult feeling is through it. We have to feel our emotions in order for them to heal and change; we have to experience the feelings…not just think and talk about them.

EXERCISE: ASK THE BODY

Take a deep, slow breath into your abdomen. Relax. Feel the sensations in your body. Take a moment to arrive here. Now pick a situation (or relationship) that's stressful. Don't pick something traumatic or deeply unsettling. Pick something at a stress level of about six or seven out of ten. Place a hand on your heart and if it feels comfortable, one on your abdomen. Now ask yourself, *How does this situation feel?* Spend a couple of minutes just listening to what comes.

If you're like most people, the first round of answers will mostly be an explanation or description of what you feel and think about this situation. The thoughts that come will be an interpretation or summary of why you feel the way you do. The first response generally comes from your mind; it's a presentation of your case and why you're right to feel the way you do.

Ask yourself again. *How does this situation feel?* This time, don't ask your head. Instead, ask your gut, your heart, or wherever feels right. Ask your body what it's like (for it) to carry this situation around.

Usually, when we ask our body what it's like to carry a problem, we get a less intellectual answer. The words that come are feeling words like "I'm hurt," or "I'm angry," or "I feel sad or heartbroken." Or sometimes, "I feel a pit in my stomach or a thickness in my chest or a fuzziness in my head." The idea at this second level is to get past your narrative about the situation, out of the head, and into the emotional and physical experience of the situation, into the body.

Notice where in your body you experience this situation and how it presents itself. Just notice without judgment. Now ask the question a third time. But rather than asking yourself how the situation feels, invite yourself to simply feel the situation and the feelings that are present. That is, do not describe, explain, or narrate them. Just feel those places in your body where sensation is present. Keep your hand on your heart and feel what your chest feels like without naming or judging it. Do the same for your gut.

The idea is not to report to yourself on how you feel, but rather to simply feel what's happening inside you, directly, without describing or explaining it to yourself. If there's a tightness in your chest, feel the tightness itself; if there's a fluttering in your belly, experience the fluttering itself; if there's an overall sense of heaviness, just feel that. Don't tell yourself about what's happening in you.

Climb Out of the Avoidance Trench

We use our excessive thinking not only as a way to not feel our feelings, but also to avoid making real changes in our life. As one client put it, "If I were to stop constantly thinking about my marriage, dissecting all the problems, I might actually have to get a divorce." While thinking about a difficult situation can certainly help us determine the next right steps to take, often we use thinking to postpone or avoid taking the actions that will create change. We devise and revise our thoughts about what's not working in our life and think up all sorts of interesting strategies for making things better—rational time lines and plans...good ideas indeed. But we get stuck there, in the thinking and planning part of the process. We fail to move on to actually *taking* the steps we spend so much time thinking about and are so good at designing. Thinking, it turns out, can be the place we get waylaid, the quicksand to our forward movement. And yet, we don't realize that it's the thinking about process itself that's keeping us stuck. Ask yourself, Are you using thinking as a way to avoid doing what needs to be done?

Choose Real Life Over Your Fictions

What is most problematic about our addiction to thinking, however, is our incessant use of thinking as a means to make sense of our life. Our mind spends most of its time threading together bits and pieces of experience, every random perception in fact, and organizing that information into a meaningful narrative that will tell the story of our life and who we are. Naturally, since we are the author, our story lines are written with ourselves as the protagonist and our own biases and conditioning steering the plot line. Creating a narrative for our life is a normal process, one designed to make meaning out of our experience. There's nothing wrong with its intention. But, in scripting the meaning out of our experience and perceptions, we lose touch with what's actually happening in reality. We end up living and believing our made-up, personal narrative on reality, which has been distorted and altered by our own psychology and conditioning. We don't see reality as it is; we see a reality of our own making, one that supports the larger movie going on inside our head. Thinking acts as a fun-house mirror, turning reality into something other than what it is.

Jane was sitting at a café when she felt a sharp pain in her foot. Immediately, thoughts flooded in about what was causing it. She decided the pain was a result of recently having gone running after not having exercised in months. From there, she concluded that she couldn't expect good things in her life if she wasn't willing to do the work for it. And that it was her choice to *not* run that was making her fat, which was why she had no boyfriend, and of course, why she would live with cats for the rest of her life. Soon, she was tangled up in a story line about how her whole life was a failure and she was to blame. Within minutes, Jane had traveled from a pain in her foot into a narrative on her inadequacy, transforming a generally pleasant present moment into a fiery state of internal agitation and self-loathing. That pain in her foot, the cause of which was unknown, and which most likely would have passed without much ado, led to a state of hopelessness and despair, an internal reality that featured Jane as a guilty and pathetic character.

In another example, Lily was taking a walk with a friend when she noticed an unfamiliar expression on her friend's face. Rather than ask the woman what was going on, if she had a toothache perhaps, she immediately decided that her friend's expression was a result of the birthday present she gave her. Undoubtedly, her gift wasn't expensive or special enough. Lily then concluded that her friend had no right to be disappointed in her because the friend hadn't even shown up for her wedding and never given her a present at all. Lily was now pissed off, resentful, and defensive, fully convinced that she was being judged for not being a good enough friend. Within moments, Lily was living in a self-constructed hell; the expression on her friend's face had been twisted into a narrative and a reality entirely of her own making. She was in a tizzy for reasons that made sense only in her own inner movie, and she still didn't have any idea what was going on with her friend's face.

As human beings, we do this with and to every situation we encounter. Something happens and we think it into something entirely unrecognizable from its original form, a projection made of our own conditioning, wounds, belief systems, memories, and everything else we've ever lived. Reality is used only as a launching pad for our own fictions. We live what we think about our life...not what it actually is.

Finally, let's consider Karen, whose narrative-making recently cost her the job she loved. Karen checks yes to eight of the eleven thinking addiction criteria. Karen is also just a normal, well-adjusted person and definitely not someone you would say is dysfunctional or delusional. She recently told me about a situation going on in which a coworker was, in Karen's story line, not doing her job the way she should have been, and the backup was creating a lot of extra work for Karen. She had spent an enormous amount of time thinking about this coworker and her resentments against her. A thousand times, Karen had replayed the things she wanted to say to her but had never actually said anything about how she perceived the situation. Using the small bits and pieces of what she knew of this woman in the office, Karen had created a convincing story about how this coworker felt entitled to do whatever she chose and, more importantly, how she assumed that Karen would pick up her slack. Karen described the woman as a "show pony" and herself as the "workhorse." In truth, Karen knew very little about this woman's history or current life situation, but nonetheless, she had a complicated and well-developed idea of what made her tick and, most importantly, what this woman thought of Karen.

At a meeting with the top players in the company, Karen's long-percolating obsessive thinking finally exploded. Utterly convinced of the rightness of her narrative, she gave voice to her thoughts and proceeded to announce the story she had written in her mind about this coworker. As it turned out, the coworker who Karen had been obsessively thinking about had a child at home who was ill. She had been doing less work, but with the blessing of management. Karen was later fired for her display of anger and disrespect.

Karen's unskillful words cost her the job, but it was her obsessive thinking that led to those unskillful words. The event happened because her thoughts had been allowed to spin off without awareness, doubt, or restraint. Ultimately, what made the situation feel unmanageable for Karen was her story of being intentionally humiliated, a workhorse to her colleague's show pony. Without even realizing it, we are all incessantly thinking up our own stories about other people, situations, and indeed ourselves. We play the roles of actor and director inside our own personal movie, the movie we've constructed and believe is really happening.

Thoughts tell us, *She is like this, He is like that,* and most importantly, *They think X, Y, and definitely Z about me.* We then go looking for evidence that confirms our story, using whatever we can find to validate our narrative while ignoring or invalidating everything that contradicts or doesn't serve it. Next, we act on the story and the meaning we've constructed in our mind. This last step is where things really start to go awry.

Our faith in thinking is predicated on the idea that our reality, our movie, is also everyone else's reality—*the* reality. And yet, the snag we run into time and again is that what we think is happening often has little to do with what anyone else thinks is happening, happened, or is true. There's no better place to witness this phenomenon than in my role as a couples therapist. What's stunning is how two people can live the same event, and yet what they think happened in that "same" event, from one person to the next, is unrecognizable. It might be the same trip to the movies, but other than the name of the movie, literally, nothing else is the same (and sometimes even the name is not the same!). What's actually happening, from one person to the next, is startlingly different. Our narratives on reality are filled with useful information—not, however, about the people, places, and things they proclaim to be about, but rather about ourselves and our own thoughts.

The whole story line we construct about our life is a matrix of our own making. Figuring out life, based solely on our personal narrative, is an exercise in futility and absurdity. We imagine we know why others do what they do, their true intentions, and of course, what they must do to improve and change. But, most of the time, when we are making these interpretations and judgments, we are not in relationship with these other people—not really. We are in a relationship with our own memories, disappointments, and beliefs, and with all the people we've ever known. Through our narratives, we are trying to confirm or correct a certain perception of ourselves, an identity we want (or don't want) to project. The stories we construct about others stem from our own projections and conditioning. Ultimately, we see who we are, not what is.

No Longer Foisting Our Reality on Others

To maintain a functioning society, we need to agree on and share certain basic realities. Right now, we would probably all agree that I am sitting at a desk in front of a computer. We would agree that it's currently raining (although you might say it's drizzling, not raining). As for the concrete elements of life, we generally find consensus without much difficulty. But, when it comes to our personal realities, our subjective experience, and the meaning we assign to every waking moment, there, we're all living in profoundly different universes. What's amazing is that each of these realities is real and true for the one who's living it, as real and true as our own reality is for us. We imagine our reality to be shared, but in fact there are billions of coexisting personal realities, billions of different worlds happening in this one physical world. We are all in our own separate theaters, witnessing different shows, and yet we imagine and behave as if we're in the same audience, watching the very same event we call real life.

When we buy into the delusion that our thoughts are the truth for everyone, we suffer, imprisoned by the certainty of our own narrative and the burden of having to make life go the way we think it should go.

Thankfully, however, it's not our job to get the world to see reality as it really exists, otherwise known as *our* reality, the way it exists inside our own mind. We don't have to carry the responsibility for promulgating the absolute truth…don't have to correct anyone else's version of what is.

Whenever we're ready, we can surrender the whole fight; our truth can be true for us while other people's truths can be true for them. We are liberated from the need to control our external world (and all those in it) when we realize that our version of the truth, which not coincidentally places us at the center of what's driving everyone and everything else, is not the truth in any fundamental sense. Our version of reality is important, but it is still just that—*our* version of reality. The sooner we accept this, the sooner we find peace.

Accepting the Still Quandary of Now

When we're thinking, the content of our thoughts is usually about something to do with the past or future. But this moment, the one happening now, is a kind of gap, poised between the two locations or two concepts: past and future. In the now, time disappears. When we're fully engaged in the present moment, thinking is not actually needed. For this reason, the present moment presents a quandary for the thinking mind: how to find a place for itself in the present moment. The mind's solution to this quandary, often, is to shift our attention to something we can think about, something still to come or, alternatively, something that's already happened.

But, when thinking and the present moment bump into each other, what transpires is a whole lot of thinking about now…thoughts on what the present moment means, whether or not we like it, and our very favorite subject, what the present moment says about ourselves. I recently gave a dear friend a heartfelt hug, just spontaneously. Upon exiting the hug, he immediately remarked, "Where's that hug coming from?" In thinking the hug into an idea, the felt experience of the hug was lost. This is how we roll as human beings, forever turning what's happening into a mental construct—thinking our way out of feeling and experiencing life.

Get Out of Your Own Way

It turns out that arriving in the present moment is a lot easier than we think and easier than our thinking mind would like us to believe. In the book *The Inner Game of Tennis*, the legendary sports psychologist Timothy Gallwey explains the importance of present moment attention in the creation of excellence and mastery. Gallwey discovered that when elite tennis players spent a lot of time thinking about what they needed to do to produce a successful swing, they were able to improve and produce that desired swing for a time, but their improvement didn't last. Soon they started thinking about their progress, what it said about their identity, why they hadn't gotten it in the past, and how they were going to keep it in the future. As a result, their success became something to not lose. Their improvement soon disappeared, and frustration returned. Gallwey then discovered that when an athlete learned to simply say "bounce" every time the ball bounced and "hit" every time the ball made contact with the racket, radical improvement occurred in the athlete's swing and, most importantly, the improvement was permanent as long as the practice was continued.[16]

The words "bounce" and "hit" were not revolutionary in and of themselves; they were simply practices Gallwey invented to help distract the athletes from thinking about all the other things that got in the way of their attention. Naming each bounce and hit allowed the tennis players to maintain present moment awareness, to stay in that point, and not get lost in their thoughts and judgments about what was happening on the court. Gallwey's students needed to distract themselves from the distraction of their own thoughts. They needed to learn how to stop thinking about how to be great, to get their mind out of the way, and to allow their body to do what it was trained to do.

Most tragically, in thinking our way out of the present moment, we deprive ourselves of the experience of joy. Thinking is the thief of joy. Trapped in our thoughts, we fail to notice the opportunities for gratitude and awe that are forever presenting themselves. We miss the moments that can inspire wonder and appreciation. We might be walking through a field of flowers, but where we *are*, really, is trapped in a conversation that happened that morning or two years ago, or maybe we're obsessing about the names of the flowers on the path, how we should get our kid into gardening, or the sixth-grade teacher who shamed us about our planting skills. But regardless of what we're thinking, the end result is that we've missed the whole field and the experience of joy and wonder it might have awakened in us. Thoughts cloud our inner sky, prevent us from seeing the beauty that resides within us and in our world. Ask yourself, *What do I miss—and what do I miss out on—because I'm busy thinking?*

PART III

Living the Inner Freedom

CHAPTER 9

The Wisdom of Not Knowing

We live in an age of reason and science. We worship information, research, and logic so much that we named our era for it: the age of information. To reason is to think, use the rational mind, understand, and make sense of our world. Over time, we've put more and more eggs in the reasoning basket, betting on thinking to save the day. The thinking mind is the road to salvation. At this moment in history, we've lost interest and, to some degree, respect, for all the other ways of knowing: bodily, intuitively, experientially, and so forth—all the ways we can know other than through thinking and logic. When I present material as a public speaker, despite three decades of professional experience with human beings and their thoughts and emotions, I am almost always asked what MRI studies or research I can offer to support my observations on human behavior. Reason and scientific proof have been anointed as our kings. Thinking, we believe, will solve whatever questions and challenges life presents. And, with technology exploding, our faith in and reverence for thinking are only intensifying.

Just by picking up this book, by being willing to put thinking itself under the microscope, you are quite literally bucking the trend of history. You are questioning what we all accept as the instrument of progress, the chosen method for making life better. To look at thinking honestly is already revolutionary. In getting curious about your own thinking process, you are potentially dethroning the thinking mind from its position as master of your universe.

Living in the Question

"The only true wisdom is in knowing we know nothing," said Socrates. A lot has changed in the twenty-five hundred years since Socrates uttered those words. Our society now seems to disagree with the great philosopher on the issue of knowing. Here, in the twenty-first century CE, we believe that we should and can know everything. Our unceasing need to know the answers along with our unwillingness to accept the unknown sit at the root of our excessive thinking.

Mystery, in our society, is not a real thing…it's a flaky or, as my friend calls it, a *woowoo* thing. Not knowing the answer is not an acceptable answer. We're taught from the time we're born that knowing is good—we are good, worthy, if we have the answers. "You should know better" is what we hear when we're young and have done something wrong. We feel shame and inadequacy when we don't have the answers: it makes us feel weak and defective, vulnerable and lost. Not knowing is a form of failure. Knowing, on the other hand, feels safe; it feels like we're in control. As a result, we do a lot of faking it, "impostering," when it comes to knowing. Simultaneously, we rush to answers that aren't true or sustainable.

But despite what we're conditioned to believe, life is forever depositing us in situations where we cannot know and don't have access to the answers we want, don't know the way forward, to say nothing of the larger not knowing—what we're all doing here, existing, in the first place. Given the frequency with which the experience of not knowing or at least not *yet* knowing shows up in life, we would be wise to learn how to inhabit it and, even better, to do so with a sense of acceptance and peace rather than judgment.

It may feel unfamiliar, unwise, and even dangerous to sit with a challenging, unresolved situation, to not know what it means, what we need to do about it, or how to get out of it. Uncomfortable though it may be, however, it behooves us to learn how to not know, to feel what it's like in the not knowing, and to await more clarity and the arrival of a path through. Living in the question, if we can drop our judgments about it, can become its very own place to reside. With practice, we can get accustomed to and even revel in not having the answers. When we offer ourselves permission to not know the answers, we can allow life to reveal what it wants to reveal in its own time, without forcing it. The questions then, remarkably, become their own destinations. What's more: we find that not knowing is a place that, if we have the courage to trust it, can deliver deeper and wiser solutions, real solutions, paths forward that are more reliable than anything we can mentally muscle our way into knowing.

The Other Side of Thinking's Illusions

The first time it was suggested to me that I stop trying to think up a solution to the situation I was trying desperately to solve, to figure it all out, it sounded like a lovely idea. But truth be told, I had no idea how to put this advice into action. Resolution, for me, had always meant understanding what was happening, what it meant, and most of all, knowing what to do about it. Resolution had always involved excessive and obsessive thinking. If I didn't want to live in anxiety and feel utterly unmoored, I had to solve the questions that were still unsolved. I had to think more, not less, about my difficulties. Living peacefully and not having the answers were incompatible; I needed a plan, a way out of the situation, not a comfy chair inside it.

But over time, I realized that despite all the thinking humanly possible, there were important questions in my life that I couldn't know and couldn't solve—not yet, anyway. This truth was unavoidable and irrefutable. I had to admit and accept that, with all my pseudo-knowing, my proposed and attempted solutions, I was still not any better off. Any knowing I had thought myself into was illusory. The more I tried to know, the more I felt like I didn't know. On the other side of that admission and acceptance, however, I found something unexpected...utter relief.

When I surrendered to living in the question, it felt like I dropped through a trapdoor. Suddenly I was deposited into the present moment; I had permission to be here, to experience what my life was like—now. I had permission to get interested in the experience of this reality and allow the answers to reveal themselves on their own time line. Just for now, I didn't have to do it all myself, didn't have to push my way through with my mind, as I had always believed and been taught. Relaxing into the questions, unexpectedly, allowed me to join a larger unfolding, a process bigger than me, and thankfully, one in which I didn't have to be responsible for controlling my life at every turn. At last, it wasn't up to only me.

The Truth Is What Is

Living in the questions, no matter how uncomfortable it might feel, is living in the truth, which, once we get the hang of it, contains its own safety and trustworthiness. The safety we experience in the truth, however, is not because we have all the answers there or because the truth is comfortable (the usual markers of safety), but rather because the truth is inarguable...because the truth is what is. Surrendering to not knowing means planting our feet in moving ground and accepting that we're in a process without a known outcome and that the process is the destination, for now.

Beyond Control Is a Fresh Version of Yourself

When we accept that we can't have all the answers, we're also inviting ourselves to be humble, to give up our identity as the one who knows, the one in control. We're acknowledging that we're not actually in control, which takes remarkable strength and courage, the courage to be honest about what's true. No matter how frightening or unfamiliar this shift in identity might feel, ultimately, it offers us the freedom to be present, to discover not only what we don't know, but also a new and more truthful version of ourselves. Ask yourself, *Where in your life are you forcing answers before they're ripe? Right now, can you let go of knowing—give yourself permission to relax in the not knowing? Can you be someone who's not in control?* You might want to journal on these questions as well.

Keeping It Simple and Kind

No matter how vested we are in thinking as the solution to life's challenges, most of us will agree that thinking tends to complicate whatever situations we apply it to. Thinking actually solidifies and expands our problems—makes them more problematic. If what we want is peace and if what we want is to be happy, however, it's a good idea to simplify our problems rather than complicate them. In the face of difficulty, or difficult people, it can be wise (oddly) to think less about what's bothering us—not more.

It's also in our best interest to replace our complicated strategizing and dissecting with something far simpler—namely, compassion. When someone else's behavior is creating a problem for us, for example, we can remind ourselves of the simple truth that this person's behavior is arising out of their own ignorance. As frustrating and hurtful as it may be, it's actually the best they can offer with the awareness and wisdom they possess at this moment (which doesn't make it right or okay). If what we're most interested in is feeling better and less bothered, we're best served by dropping the figuring out and, instead, injecting a dose of compassion into our inner experience and response. We can remind ourselves that this other person, *our* problem, wants the very same things we want—happiness, safety, and to not suffer. We share these longings with the source of our discontent. This other person wants these things, even when the way they're going about is unlikable and counterproductive. Our own suffering diminishes, paradoxically, when we keep our response as simple and compassionate as possible and open our heart to the larger humanness at play.

Regardless of whether we can find compassion for this other, it is an act of profound compassion—for ourselves—to stop trying to figure out and fix everything we disagree with, every problem we see, and stop trying to get others to understand the error of their ways. Grounding our attention in kindness and simplicity, resisting the urge to go up into our head, into thought and judgment, improves not only how we feel but also the situation—far more than any mental gymnastics ever will or can.

Trying to Unlock the Door to Peace—with a Banana

When a new client shows up in my office, I usually ask what they hope to get out of or discover in our work together. Essentially, why they're there. The answer, frequently, has something to do with craving a sense of internal peace, but not being able to find it in any reliable way. Since we believe that thinking can solve all our problems, it makes sense then to think that thinking should also be the answer to the problem of our longing for peace. And indeed, sadly, we believe we can think our way into internal peace.

While thinking may give us a pseudo-sense of control, thinking as a path to peace doesn't work; thinking doesn't deliver the peace we crave. If I had a nickel for every time I heard someone say, "When I don't try to figure it all out, I'm happier, and things just go better" (or something similar), I'd be a very wealthy woman. We can think ourselves out of peace for sure, but we can't, no matter how hard we try, think our way into it.

In reality, the mind is not always the appropriate tool to improve our life. The mind, in fact, is sometimes the worst tool we can pull out of the shed, not just because it's unhelpful, a bit like using a banana to open a lock, but ultimately, because it's detrimental to what we really want. There's a question I often ask my clients: *Do you want to be right, or do you want to be happy?* This question speaks directly to the dilemma: what the mind can offer versus what we really desire. The mind can prove, with all its clever thoughts, why we're right in any situation, but none of that thinking or proving will result in our real goal: to feel better—to be happy. When it comes to internal peace, what's needed is often something entirely different than mind—something not made of thoughts. The path to peace is rarely paved with thoughts, and far more often paved with surrender.

When Surrender Dawns

Too often, the term "surrender" is misunderstood, boiled down to a few affirmations about letting go and then misused as a tepid self-help instruction. Too often, surrender is seen as defeat or failure, something to avoid at all costs. And, like everything else, surrender is misunderstood as something we can *do* with our minds. Surely there must be a strategy, a way of thinking about surrender that leads to surrender. But surrender is a different animal than anything we're used to. True surrender defies logic, the rational mind, and everything else, which is precisely why it's so profound and powerful.

Our mind attempts to control everything it comes in contact with—and everything it doesn't—ostensibly, to try to keep us safe, make us happy, and ensure that our lives will get better. Our mind will resist, reject, ignore, push against, and keep maneuvering to change situations we don't want or don't like. But at some point in our life, every one of us encounters a situation that rocks the foundation of who we are and what we think we can survive—something that pushes us past our limits. Sometimes it's a situation we've been living with for a long time that reaches a breaking point, and sometimes it's a sudden event that over-whelms us and for which our usual coping strategies are useless. What these experiences share is the power to bring us to our knees, figuratively and often literally as well. And, the power to change us.

For most of us, there comes a situation (or person) that proves beyond a shadow of a doubt that it's not up to us—we're not in charge. A moment arrives when we know at a cellular level that all the figuring out in the world is not going to help us and some other unknown path is called for. Sooner or later, our thinking mind is defeated; we lose the fight. Surrender begins here, where all other mental strategies end. Surrender happens when we finally get it…get that we can't mentally muscle our way into a different reality. The experience of surrender dawns when we give up all hope of being able to control what is.

But surrender is not another strategy, not a no-strategy strategy. It is the absence of all strategies. At the point of surrender, we accept the fact that all the strategies have failed, that we're fresh out of strategies and don't know what comes next. At the point of surrender, we know that we cannot think our way out of not knowing. We don't know whether what's to come will be better or worse, more comfortable or more uncomfortable, but what we do know is that we can't do life the way we've been doing it.

Surrender happens when surrender can no longer *not* happen. It presents itself when control falls away and takes us with it. The path to surrender can be excruciating, but when it finally does arrive, it's often accompanied by a great sense of relief and peace. It's not as if our reality remarkably gets better or easier, but we feel better and more at ease when we finally acknowledge that the mental gymnastics are not working and are not going to work, that whatever we're trying to do is not possible— not this way. In surrender, there's clarity and relief. At last, we can stop demanding of ourselves that we be able to figure it out, make it happen, change it. What comes then, surprisingly, is a feeling of deep relaxation, an inner softening, when we turn the situation over to Reality with a capital R, to the inscrutable mystery that is life, or to anything, really, that's not us. On our knees, paradoxically, is where we find our remission from suffering.

When we surrender, we give up, but not in the way we think of giving up. We don't give up hoping the situation will change. Rather, we give up the idea that we *should* or *can* control it, can make it change. We give up the belief that we, with all our great ideas, cleverness, and planning, can make reality different than what it is. As much as we are conditioned to never give up, the fact is, giving up the belief that we are in charge and that our mind can save us from anything is sometimes the only way to ever find real peace.

Still, we don't trust that anything other than our mind can take care of us show us the way, which is why surrender feels so unthinkable. But we surrender because we have to, because we've exhausted every other option. And luckily for us, surrender does not require our faith or approval; it doesn't ask us to sign off on its arrival. When we finally do let go of the reins, acknowledge our mind's defeat, a profound space opens up, and an opportunity appears. Namely, the opportunity to experience the support of a larger source—to feel ourselves being guided or buoyed by something other than just our own mind. Some people call that source grace, but it doesn't matter what you call it. Once you experience it, you can never not know it's here. In the space of surrender, we can experience life carrying us, leading us where we need to go, even if we have no idea where that is. In surrender, we stop feeling so alone.

Opening to Surrender's Discoveries

So why talk about surrender if it's something that just happens, that we can't actually make happen or think into fruition? Do we simply wait for surrender's unwelcome yet welcome arrival, or is there anything we can do to encourage its arrival?

It's true that the mind can't think or muscle its way into surrender, can't *do* surrender like it does everything else. Nonetheless, surrender is something that we can invite into our lives. Ironically, surrender is simpler than the mind can fathom—too simple, in fact, for the mind to comprehend—or tolerate. To practice surrender, we start right here, right now, exactly where we are. We drop into this very moment. We see and feel what's here…the sensations in the body, the breath, sounds, emotions, and thoughts (without getting engaged in their content). We drop into what's here now, without adding, taking away, or doing anything else with it. We invite surrender when we open to now without any resistance to what we discover—without pushing anything away. Surrender is stepping into this moment—exactly as it is.

EXERCISE: AND THIS TOO

Take a deep breath. Relax. Turn your attention from outside to inside. Tune in to the sensations in your body. Now, notice whether there's an emotion present, something strong or perhaps a more wallpaper-like, background emotion. Don't go deeply into it; don't dive into its story; just feel the sense of that emotion.

Ask yourself, *Can I completely relax with what's here, without pushing anything away? If not, what's in the way? What's here that I think I cannot possibly relax with or into?* Now relax even with that; relax with whatever you think is in the way of relaxing. If there's further resistance, relax with that resistance too. Adopt an attitude of "and this too" with everything included. Feel what it's like to profoundly relax, to truly let go.

Giving up resistance to this very moment is at the root of surrender. Surrender is the practice of letting go into this moment, with all that it contains. When we invite ourselves to fully relax into this moment, to stop trying to control it, stop bracing against it, stop pushing it away, we are inviting the process that brings us the deepest peace.

Thankfully, when we have no choice but to surrender, to give up all delusions of control, we then notice that life is happening without our doing anything to make it happen. When we let go, entirely, we are suddenly in touch with how we're being supported and carried by life. It is through the doorway of surrender that we sense the presence of something larger than just ourselves, something that's guiding us even as we desperately try to steer the wheel. We feel the sense of being lived rather than being the one who's doing the living and managing life. We can then relax and know, from a place not made of thought, that it's safe to let go, take our hands off the wheel, and let ourselves be led. Once again, the paradox prevails: when we realize we're not in charge, this is when we feel most well—and most safe. Thankfully, there is so much more to us, and our universe, than we can ever know.

CHAPTER 10

Beyond a Self That Thinks

At the heart of every thought and indeed all thinking is a deep and visceral sense of a *me*. We know ourselves as the *me* who's coming up with the thoughts, the thinker, and also the *me* that our thoughts are trying to protect and promote. Everything our mind is busy doing, in one way or another, is an attempt to advance our *me*'s safety, success, and survival. Thoughts—most of them, anyway—are about keeping our *me* intact: physically, mentally, emotionally, and in every other way imaginable. How does this moment feel to *me*? Is it doing something positive for *me*? Does *me* like it or not like it? Is it comfortable for *me*? It's not that we're all raging narcissists; it's just the human condition. There exists a built-in self-centeredness and self-protectiveness that's part of how we evolved.

Copernicus may have proven that the sun is at the center of our solar system, but in our own mind, while that may be interesting information, it's not how we operate or experience life. We know that fact about the sun to be true, but like everything else, that fact lives inside our own mind, which sits at the real epicenter of our personal universe. Our little *me* is our real sun, the one around which everything else revolves and through which everything else is viewed.

The *Me* at the Center of the Universe

At the center of our relentless thinking is the subject we imagine to be the most important one in existence: our self—*me*. Just in the last five minutes, we've all probably had at least twenty thoughts about what our little *me* wants, needs, fears, likes, doesn't like, is getting, and is not getting. And furthermore, we believe that this *me* is real and solid—something that exists in its own right. It's our job to keep this solid self alive and well, which is what we're so busy thinking about.

When we think of our self, we imagine an entity that's housed inside this body, something we could find if we went looking for it. Take a moment and investigate your own experience. *Where do you experience your self living inside you? Where is it actually located? Is this self behind your eyes, in your mouth, your belly? How do you imagine this self?*

Once you've physically located where your *self* resides and maybe what it looks like, ask yourself the next question: *What is your self actually made of?* You might use the inquiry, *Who am I?* Or perhaps, *What am I?* Every now and again, stop and ask yourself this question: *Who or what is this self I am always referring to?*

If you took the time to engage in this process, you probably came up with a list of words, roles, descriptions, and ideas to define your *self*. You might have thought about your gender or ethnicity; I'm a woman, a transgender person, a Brazilian or African American. Or perhaps you defined your *self* through the interpersonal roles you play: I am a mother, a friend, a sister. Or your profession: I am a dentist, a teacher, a photographer. Or maybe your religion: I am a Jew, a Christian. Maybe your sense is linked to your sexual inclinations: I am a lesbian, a bisexual person. Your *I am* might also have been followed by a trauma you experienced: I am a rape survivor, or a widow. Or perhaps by a set of beliefs or political affiliation: I am a democrat, a socialist, or a feminist. Maybe you identify as a set of characteristics: I am a funny, quirky, or pessimistic person. Or maybe who you *are* is what you do in your free time: I am a surfer, a horseback rider, a crossword puzzle master. You get the point.

But if you look closely, everything you think you are, fundamentally, is something you do, believe in, think, or enjoy or a role you play in relation to others. Everything you believe you *are*, boiled down, is just a description of who you are. Everything you imagine as your fundamental *self* turns out to be something *about* yourself. So, the question begs, what actually *is* your *self*, what is it made of—this solid entity for which all these descriptions exist and around which all of your thinking transpires?

The Physical Self

For most people, the *self*, at the most basic level, is the body. *I am my body.* Our physical form is something solid and tangible that we can point to, something that feels like part of our basic identity. From a young age, we realize that we alone are the ones who experience pain when our finger touches the hot stove, while our sister who didn't touch the stove doesn't feel that burn. Similarly, it's our leg that breaks when we fall—no one else's leg. What happens to our body is something that seems to separate and differentiate us from other people and other bodies. And therefore, something that makes us who we are. Furthermore, when our body disappears, so do our personality traits, our words, and our memories, all the things that we think of as *me*. If there's no body, there's no self. Then, in essence, we are our body.

And yet, if we consider our body at various times throughout our life, we find that this solid thing we call our self is, in fact, an entirely different body depending on when we are doing the considering. The body we inhabit now is not the same as it was when we were a child, twenty or ten years ago, or even yesterday. It's not only the outside of our body that looks completely different, but also our cells and organs that are in a constant process of dying and being reborn. We are literally not made of the same elements physically as we were at birth, or even last year. Our physical form is always in flux.

To complicate matters, we are also aware of our body. We can say we have a pain in our foot, which would imply we are not that foot. Something beyond the body is conscious of what's happening in the body. And, we can lose whole parts of our body, have a foot or a liver removed and still exist, without losing who we are. So, if we can lose parts of this thing called body, can we fundamentally *be* this entity called body?[17]

The Thinking Self

If we are not the body, we must be our thoughts then. What's going on in our mind must contain our essential nature, our *me-ness*. The problem, however, is that thoughts are also changing from moment to moment, and no thought sticks around for very long. How can we *be* something that is always changing? And furthermore, we can witness our thoughts; something in us is aware of their content as well as their appearance and disappearance. Therefore, who we are must be bigger or more expansive than thoughts; something must sit behind even thoughts. We can't be what we can witness.

No matter where we go looking for this *self*, our *self*, the little *me*, we uncover only processes of change. There appears to be no actual *self* we can find, touch, or locate within our head, heart, or anywhere else. Our *self* must be continually reestablished and reassembled, culled together from memory, thoughts, and present conditions. We can talk *about* the self, describe it, but that appears to be as close as we can get.

And yet, despite the evidence, we continue to believe and invest in a *me* that's constant and unchanging, a solid, real somebody deserving of our undying loyalty and protection. We are so convinced of this truth, in fact, that we spend our entire lives defending this concept called *me*.

Beyond the Solidity of Self

It can feel not only counterintuitive but also dangerous to turn away from thoughts that are designed to protect and defend ourselves. Can we recognize that this entity we call *self*, this *me* we're thinking about all the time, whose experiences we're always trying to change and control, is not a solid identity, not something that exists in some physical place, but rather, another concept constructed out of other thoughts, feelings experience, and memories? When we see through this *self*, see it for the tapestry of thoughts that it really is, our attachment to the subject of our thinking begins to loosen, and with it, the thinking itself. We can wear even our own self with a sense of lightness and ease.

The other day I was sitting in a meeting with a dreadfully boring speaker. I was not only struggling to pay attention, but I also started to feel agitated and began planning my escape. I noticed that I was feeling extremely uncomfortable and bothered, as if I were being harmed in some way by this speaker and this experience. I felt like I had to get out of the room or my head would explode, as if I were enduring a form of mental and emotional torture. And then the following line of questioning popped into my mind: *Who is it that's being tortured by this experience? Who is this happening to?* And furthermore, *Where exactly is this self that's being bored at this moment?*

I could acknowledge that boredom was arising, but the belief or conviction that there was this little *me* trapped somewhere inside this body that was being bored, bothered, and imprisoned seemed far less plausible.

In the middle of the meeting, I spontaneously burst out laughing (which thankfully, momentarily spiced up the meeting). It's not that I suddenly found the speaker interesting or funny (he wasn't) but I noticed that my resistance to being there dropped on a scale of one to ten from a ten to about a three, from code red to code yellow. This boredom was still happening, but I suddenly didn't have to fight against it anymore. What changed was that this experience was no longer happening to a little *me* that I needed to protect with my resistance and anger and impending flight. In an instant, I could see that my mind was operating from the idea of a *self*—a *me* who this experience was happening *to*, that was being victimized by this boredom.

In my desire to flee, there also existed, I realized, a background assumption that my *me* should always be comfortable and psychologically happy, which was, of course, being threatened by this speaker. My *me*, in my imagination, was entitled to a comfort that was being disrupted and denied. But, without the sense of and belief in a solid and real *me* to which this was happening, and simultaneously, absent the assumption that this imaginary *self* deserved to be comfortable at all times, the meeting itself, remarkably, became bearable. Still dull, but bearable. What I discovered was that I could tolerate the feelings of boredom that were arising, the lack of interest that was undeniable. But what I couldn't tolerate and, in another minute, what would have had me running out of the room, was the idea that this experience was being done to *me*—that I was being victimized by it. And, simultaneously, that I deserved a different and better experience, of which I was being deprived. Without the certainty of a self at the center of that experience, the experience could happen without it having to happen to me.

EXERCISE: YOU VS. NOT YOU

Close your eyes and take a few deep breaths. Tune in to the sensations inside your body. Spend a few moments just feeling inside your body. Now tune in to the places where your body is making contact with the chair and floor. While still holding this internal awareness, open your attention to include the sensation of the air against your skin. Pause and feel. Go slowly. Now notice the space around your body and throughout the room. Pause. Gradually expand your attention to include the space outside the room, moving out as far as you can imagine—out to the galaxy and beyond. Hold the awareness, simultaneously, of the inside experience and the outside experience.

Now, with your eyes still closed, sense whether there is any distinction between your awareness of the internal and the external; notice whether a boundary exists at the edge of your body where awareness experiences a switch from inside to outside—from you to not you. Notice how, through the eyes of awareness, inside and outside, you and not you are just ideas. Notice how, in your direct experience, there is no separation between self and not self. What if there is only one thing, awareness, within which what you call you and what you call everything else, is simply appearing? Contemplate this possibility.

Realizing that we've been protecting and defending a self that is not real, at least not in the way we had believed it to be real, a self that is itself a thought, is like discovering we're inside a matrix, a mind-constructed universe that doesn't exactly exist, except as a structure inside our own mind. This newfound awareness about our illusionary *self* can be frightening and disorienting at first. It's a complete paradigm shift in the way we see everything, our entire way of existing. It takes a while to even be able to stay with this new awareness, to keep hold of it. And rest assured, our little *me* will fight like mad to come back and reclaim its place at the center of our attention, reassert its importance and convince us of its absolute solidity and realness. Our mind will reject any notion that we are not or don't possess a separate self.

Despite the initial fear, disorientation, and rudderless-ness that come with this awakening, as we contemplate it, and test-drive it, if you will, we notice that our relentless thinking *about* and in service to our *self* begins to wane. It becomes less urgent and enticing to protect and defend something we can see through and can see as another thought. Once we discover the thought that precedes all other thoughts, the first thought, the *I* thought, the whole game shifts—life changes. As the certainty of a solid and definable self unravels, our compulsion to keep thinking about it, and indeed keep thinking it into existence, loses traction and excessive thinking rapidly diminishes. As a result, the cacophony in our mind becomes increasingly quiet. This is the inner peace we're all seeking, and it is the basis for living a good life.

CHAPTER 11

A Good Life, the Afterthought

Over these last ten chapters, we've been investigating our universally shared love affair with thought. We've turned the lens on our addiction to thinking, the various patterns in which our addiction manifests, and how these patterns cause anxiety, stress, and suffering. So too, we've examined the deeper causes of excessive thinking: on a psychological, sociological, and spiritual level—what keeps us hooked and makes thoughts so sticky. We've explored our infatuation, reverence, and identification with thought, our undying faith in the thinking process as the solution to all of life's challenges and mysteries.

Throughout this process, I hope you've discovered, at an experiential and not just an intellectual level, that you are *not* the voice yammering in your head—and furthermore, that you've come to identify more and more with the *you* who is aware of your thoughts rather than the thoughts themselves. I hope you've also discovered that you can be the master of your own attention—that is, choose which thoughts you pay attention to and which you decide to let pass.

The exercises in this book are designed to help you cultivate a home base from which to observe and navigate the choppy waters of your mind—a place within you that is separate from thought. You may have developed a healthy and robust suspicion of the certainty of your thoughts and an equally robust skepticism of the idea that figuring life out is the solution to all its challenges. This is a good thing. The exercises and inquiries in this book are meant to be practiced again and again, with new discoveries along the way; they are not riddles to be solved and then moved on from. Awareness is a way of living—a path, not a destination. I invite you to live with these practices and questions, to continue using them as a doorway into the quiet spaces between your thoughts, into peace and the wonder of being fully present.

What Happens Once You're Free from Thought

Put simply, awareness is the key to a good life. When we become conscious of our own thoughts, what they're up to, and how we're responding, then we can free ourselves internally, which is the most radical form of freedom that exists. Our emotional state and behavior are no longer a roller coaster, putting us at the mercy of shifting situations and the challenges that come and go; our well-being no longer depends on the momentary contents of life. When we don't have to take a ride on every thought that rolls through our mind, our mood becomes increasingly more stable and reliable. Our attention is no longer shackled to the thoughts coming and going. Able to stay present with what's happening inside and out, we discover a sustainable equanimity, a sense of spaciousness that replaces the clutter of thoughts. We experience a state of being that is steady and serene, right here in the midst of life.

In addition, when we stop believing that our thoughts are true, certain, and inherently important, we no longer have to accept their direction and obey them. As the witness to thought, we stop being its prisoner; we are released from the dysfunctional computer inside our head. Furthermore, when we stop holding ourselves responsible for the content of thought, we can relinquish the burdensome task of having to police and control what's appearing in our mind.

Simultaneously, when our emotional state and behavior are no longer controlled by every thought that appears, we are free to conduct ourselves in a manner that aligns with our integrity; we can start being the person we want to be in the world. The ability to observe thoughts without being driven by them allows us to live with intention, in sync with our real values. We start consciously directing the path of our life. At any moment, we may be flooded with negative thoughts, blindsided by irrational thoughts, inundated with obsessive thoughts, but instead of having to engage with or act on such thoughts, we can witness what our mind is doing and still remain present to our deeper values and intentions. There is space and time (glorious space and glorious time) between the thoughts and our response. As a result, we can sustain the awareness to ask, *Who do I want to be in this present moment? Who do I want to be in the face of these thoughts? What relationship with and response to these thoughts will serve my larger intentions, build character that's in line with my deeper values?*

Empowered with a newfound sense of presence, we gain the privilege of choice—the choice to be who and how we want to be in our life. No longer compelled to respond to every thought that passes through our mind, we are awarded with mental space, the capacity to pause and see our thoughts, and then determine our behavior. Moments happen in slower motion, as if time were expanding in front of us. The muscle of awareness provides us with a different experience of time and with perspective and distance, all of which allow us to act from a place of integrity and wisdom. The result is that we build self-esteem and start respecting ourselves, that we like how we are showing up in the world. We find that we can trust ourselves and rely on our own steadiness. Breaking free from addictive thinking gives us back the opportunity to be our best self.

Realizing that our truth is just *our* truth, not *the* truth, that our experience is not *right* in some absolute sense, liberates us from the burden of having to correct everyone else's reality, force other people's experiences into alignment with our own. When we let go of the belief that what we see is *what is*, and we awaken to the fact that there are infinite *what ises*, all of which can be true, then we are free—free to allow other people's experiences to exist and to let other people be as they are. Understanding that our truth is just one of an infinite number of truths (constructed out of our conditioning, life experiences, traumas, and all the rest) allows us to hold our truth with a degree of lightness, to wear it like a loose garment. Indeed, everything we experience feels lighter and less fraught with anxiety and the need for defense. At last, other people's versions of reality can coexist with ours without threatening us. We can even get curious and listen to other people's realities, maybe for the first time. The rightness of our reality no longer relies on universal agreement or confirmation. "And, not but" becomes our paradigm for living. When we are no longer the authority on what's right, but instead the authority on what's right for us, right now, then at the most profound level, body, mind, and spirit can finally relax.

A New Kind of Freedom

So far, I've been identifying the changes and different freedoms that come with awareness, particularly awareness of thought. We've looked at some life-altering changes, and still, there's more liberation to be found. When we give up the belief that every situation and problem can be figured out with more thought—when we really *get it,* that thinking more about a problem does not guarantee us a resolution or a sense of peace—then we can confidently jump off the train of excessive thinking. We can allow ourselves to not know, to not have all the answers—and thus to stop all the obsessive figuring out. When we wake up to the fact that thinking may actually be making us more unhappy—creating more problems, not less—we are released from the compulsion to keep thinking. We can let ourselves be off duty.

At Last, Seeing What Is

The process of becoming aware of our thoughts allows us to see our habitual, incessant, and, until now, unconscious compulsion to tell ourselves stories and construct narratives out of every moment, which we confuse with absolute reality. Once we see our propensity to create our own personal meaning out of what is, we can see through the stories, recognizing them for the self-made fictions they are. Once we see through them, our stories unravel and lose their meaning, and we stop confusing our personal narratives with the truth. The movies in our head can then be just that—movies in our head. We can make our way back to the simplicity of what is, to just what's happening, with nothing added onto or into it. Aware of our own story-making, aware of what we *do* with reality, we are free, perhaps for the first time, to start living what is. We then enter a relationship with reality as it exists, before we reshape it, rewrite it, turn it into something about ourselves. We experience what's here directly, without ourselves in the way. This is the invitation into reality that exceeds all others.

Remembering Our Inherent Well-Being

When our attention is bouncing from thought to thought, which usually means from problem to problem, we are in a state of dissatisfaction, needing something to make this moment different or better. As we know by now, thoughts specialize in what is problematic; the voice in our head, more often than not, is telling us what's missing, what should be happening that isn't, what needs to be fixed. But when we take a step back from thoughts, when who we are is no longer the voice in our head but rather the awareness that hears it, we drop into a new reality. The contents of the problems our thoughts are reminding us of may not have changed or gone away, but the place from which we are looking at them has shifted. We are no longer inside of or merged with those problems; they're here, but we are separate from them. The result is that we gain access to a place of reliable well-being. We feel a sense of contentment that is remarkably not reliant upon the situations in our life. When we drop below thoughts, below thinking, we discover a state of being that is fundamentally well, that lacks nothing, even when the contents of our life are not how we want them to be. We uncover a sense of peace that surpasses all the mind's understanding.

Arriving in the Present Moment

When lost in thought, when busy thinking, we are not present, not here in this moment. Our life is happening, but without us in it. Thoughts kidnap our attention and send us into the past or the future or sometimes into a narrative about what's happening here. In the process, we miss out on what's right in front of us, just as I missed out on that beautiful day in the park I described at the start of this book.

Awakening to the fact that our relentless thinking is a distraction from the present moment, and therefore its own impediment to happiness and peace, allows us to stop naively entering the rabbit hole of thinking. We stop believing in thinking as inherently useful and positive. When we are no longer distracted by thinking around the clock, we start to feel more present, more here. Our attention is available to focus on what's happening in front of us and inside us. We feel our senses coming alive and experience ourselves as embodied. We become a whole, grounded being, not just a head tethered to nothing, floating about in the world. We start noticing our environment, becoming aware of joys, pleasures, and emotions we would have missed. We become aware of our own presence. At last, we get to be where we are, in our actual life as it's happening. Just as a picture syncs up with its frame, we sync up with the frame of our own life.

When thinking is no longer our constant state and thoughts are not incessantly hijacking our attention, the present moment turns from gray to Technicolor, from invisible to visible. The present moment becomes something that's alive and actually unfolding in front of us. No longer disappeared inside our heads, we get a seat inside life. Now becomes a lived experience. When we change our relationship with thought, we enter our life.

Who Are You, Anyway?

When we think of who we are, what our self is fundamentally made of, we typically think of the roles we play in life, what we do and how others would identify us. So too, we think of ourselves as a synthesis of our thoughts and opinions, what we agree and disagree with, what we believe in, stand for, and all the rest. At the same time, we imagine our essence is comprised of our memories, joys, wounds, intentions, intuitions, and all the experiences we've ever lived through. And yet, when examined closely, all of these component parts fall short in capturing who we *really* are. These defining elements are *about* us, and therefore useful in describing us, but ultimately, they do not capture the pith of who we are. These descriptors and narratives tell a story about us, but they cannot capture our essence, that which has always been here, unchanging, from the time we were born until now, even as everything else *about* us—our thoughts, beliefs, experiences, bodies, friends, jobs, and everything else—has changed.

There is a sense of being within each of us, an awareness, a presence, a consciousness, or whatever you wish to call it, that remains still, unchanging, steady, calm, and aware of everything happening inside and outside of us. This being *is* who we are, and it is what is always here. This self before and below thought is our fundamental self.

When we unhook from thought, we take a step back into a place of just being, where we are whole and lack nothing, a state in which *all is well*. Before, below, and beyond thought (depending on how you imagine it), a state of profound well-being exists. Our worldly situations still exist, but their ability to disrupt our fundamental equanimity has dissolved. When we drop into the silence below the noise of thoughts, the stillness behind the chaos of mind, we discover peace.

Embarking on a Process

Your thoughts and your relationship with thoughts have taken a lifetime to form—generated and encouraged by familial and societal conditioning of the strongest order. Your excessive thinking did not start today, nor is it likely to end today. The awareness and liberation I describe in this book is an ongoing process, not a destination, a process that to some degree is never completed. That moment I spoke of in the introduction to this book, when my lens suddenly turned on its axis and I could see my obsessive thoughts and how I was choosing to engage with them—ultimately choosing to inflict my own suffering—was not actually just a moment.

There was nothing sudden about my awakening, although the stunning clarity of it felt like it appeared suddenly. Truth be told, I had been practicing awareness for many years until that awakening dawned.

The new awareness I describe does not usually come in a flash, all at once, but rather many times in little awakenings, little glimpses. We wake up out of thinking, and then we fall back asleep, back into the dream of thoughts. Then we wake up again and then again. Little by little, we discover that we are awake and conscious of thoughts more often than we're not. We feel ourselves increasingly here, in the present moment, not lost in thought. Spaces between thoughts start to appear more regularly, and we inhabit them with greater ease. Slowly, the balance shifts, and excessive thinking ceases to be our default way of living. We take up residence in the witness seat rather than occasionally visiting it. With practice, a state of being that is peaceful and spacious becomes our normal resting state.

This internal peace I speak of is a deep well-being within you, a well-being that does not rely upon the contents of your life situation or your thoughts. This well-being is always here, always available to you. Just as you know the sun is always present even when it's hidden behind the clouds, so too this fundamental well-being is always with you. The moment you drop out of thought and drop into awareness, into the embodied presence that is your real nature, you come home, into peace. There exists, under all the thoughts and thinking, a *you* that is fundamentally and unshakably well. May you find your way home and discover a peace that surpasses all understanding.

Acknowledgments

It is difficult to capture in words the appreciation I feel for those who have contributed to the creation of this book. There are too many to thank, a lifetime of people who have nourished my spirit, heart, and mind, and thereby watered the seeds of what I write. So, I have chosen just a few helpful beings who were part of this particular project.

A big thank you to my editors Elizabeth Hollis Hansen and Jennifer Holder. Your thoughtfulness, deep listening, and hard work shaped this book into something that could truly be of service. Thinking about thinking, together, has been fun.

I am deeply grateful to Stephan Bodian, for your generous offer to contribute the foreword. Your wisdom and kindness have helped expand my vision and confirm my direct experience.

To Vesela Simik, I am lucky to have your eyes on my work. Your input is always helpful and always moves me forward.

To my dear sisters in friendship, Shauna Storey, Bronwen Davis, Melissa McCool, and Karen Greenberg. Each one of you, in your own unique ways, lights up my life and tethers me to what matters.

Thank you to Jan Bronson, for always being on my side and for encouraging my ideas to bloom.

To Frederic, thank you for being the copilot in our wonderful family and life. As a writer, you get the process, and I am thankful for the ground and humor that you bring to everything.

And to my girls, Juliet and Gretchen, my biggest joy, my heart. Every day I'm awed by my great fortune; I will never understand nor be able to confine to language my gratitude for getting to be your mom.

Endnotes

1   American Psychiatric Association, *Diagnostic and Statistical Manual of Mental Disorders Fifth Edition* (Washington, DC: American Psychiatric Publishing, 2013).

2   Mark Epstein, *Thoughts Without a Thinker* (New York: Basic Books, 2013).

3   Eckhart Tolle, "Breaking Addiction to Negative Thinking," February 18, 2018, accessed September 2019, https://www.youtube .com/watch?v=j91ST2gtR44.

4   Neringa Antanaityte, "Mind Matters: How to Effortlessly Have More Positive Thoughts," tLEX Institute, accessed May 2020, https://tlexinstitute.com/how-to-effortlessly-have-more -positive-thoughts.

5   Deepak Chopra, "Why Meditate?" March 5, 2017, accessed December 15, 2019, https://www.deepakchopra.com/articles /why-meditate.

6   Maria Millet, "Challenge Your Negative Thoughts," Michigan State University MSU Extension, March 31, 2017, https://www.canr.msu .edu/news/challenge_your_negative_thoughts.

7   Rick Hanson, *Hardwiring Happiness: The New Brain Science of Contentment, Calm, and Confidence* (New York: Harmony Books, 2016), 42–43.

8   Kyle Benson, "The Magic Relationship Ratio, According to Science," The Gottman Institute, October 4, 2017, https://www .gottman.com/blog/the-magic-relationship-ratio-according-science.

9   Hanson, *Hardwiring Happiness*, 42–43.

10 Tolle, "Breaking Addiction to Negative Thinking," https://www
   .youtube.com/watch?v=j91ST2gtR44.

11 From the teachings of Mooji. www.mooji.com.

12 Emily Carlson, "Bacterial 'Glue' Is One of Nature's Stickiest
   Substances," LiveScience, February 8, 20102, accessed April 26,
   2020, https://www.livescience.com/18381-bacterial-glue-stickiest-
   substance-nsf-ria.html.

13 Sally M. Winston and Martin N. Self, *Overcoming Unwanted
   Intrusive Thoughts* (Oakland, CA: New Harbinger Publications,
   2017).

14 Steve Bradt, "Wandering Mind Not a Happy Mind," *Harvard
   Gazette*, Harvard University, November 11, 2010, accessed
   December 11, 2019, https://news.harvard.edu/gazette/story/2010
   /11/wandering-mind-not-a-happy-mind.

15 Adyashanti. *The Most Important Thing* (Louisville, CO: Sounds
   True, 2019), 142.

16 Timothy Gallwey, *The Inner Game of Tennis* (New York: Random
   House, 1997), 7–8.

17 From the teachings of Mooji. www.mooji.com.

Nancy Colier is a psychotherapist, interfaith minister, author, and public speaker. A longtime student of Eastern spirituality, she is a thought leader on mindfulness, well-being, and digital life. Featured on *Good Morning America, Fox & Friends, RT America,* in *The New York Times,* and other media, Colier is also a regular blogger for *Psychology Today* and *HuffPost.* She is author of *The Power of Off, Inviting a Monkey to Tea,* and *Getting Out of Your Own Way.* Colier resides in New York City, NY. You can learn more about her at https://www.nancycolier.com.

Foreword writer **Stephan Bodian** is a teacher in the non-dual wisdom tradition of Zen and Advaita, a pioneer in the integration of Eastern wisdom and Western psychology, and an internationally recognized expert on meditation and mindfulness. You can learn more about him at https://www.stephanbodian.org.

Real change *is* possible

For more than forty-five years, New Harbinger has published proven-effective self-help books and pioneering workbooks to help readers of all ages and backgrounds improve mental health and well-being, and achieve lasting personal growth. In addition, our spirituality books offer profound guidance for deepening awareness and cultivating healing, self-discovery, and fulfillment.

Founded by psychologist Matthew McKay and Patrick Fanning, New Harbinger is proud to be an independent, employee-owned company. Our books reflect our core values of integrity, innovation, commitment, sustainability, compassion, and trust. Written by leaders in the field and recommended by therapists worldwide, New Harbinger books are practical, accessible, and provide real tools for real change.

newharbingerpublications

MORE BOOKS from
NEW HARBINGER PUBLICATIONS

**QUIET YOUR MIND
AND GET TO SLEEP**

Solutions to Insomnia for
Those with Depression,
Anxiety, or Chronic Pain

978-1572246270 / US $22.95

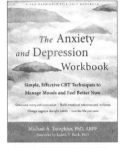

**THE ANXIETY AND
DEPRESSION
WORKBOOK**

Simple, Effective CBT
Techniques to Manage Moods
and Feel Better Now

978-1684036141 / US $24.95

ACT DAILY JOURNAL

Get Unstuck and Live
Fully with Acceptance and
Commitment Therapy

978-1684037377 / US $18.95

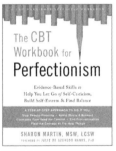

**THE CBT WORKBOOK
FOR PERFECTIONISM**

Evidence-Based Skills to Help
You Let Go of Self-Criticism,
Build Self-Esteem, and
Find Balance

978-1684031535 / US $24.95

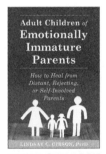

**ADULT CHILDREN
OF EMOTIONALLY
IMMATURE PARENTS**

How to Heal from
Distant, Rejecting, or
Self-Involved Parents

978-1626251700 / US $18.95

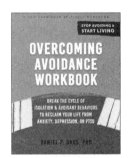

**OVERCOMING
AVOIDANCE WORKBOOK**

Break the Cycle of Isolation and
Avoidant Behaviors to Reclaim
Your Life from Anxiety,
Depression, or PTSD

978-1684035663 / US $24.95